AI and Creative Writing

Graeme Harper
Editor

AI and Creative Writing

palgrave
macmillan

Editor
Graeme Harper
Donna & Walt Young Honors
College
Oakland University
Rochester, MI, USA

ISBN 978-3-031-99100-4 ISBN 978-3-031-99101-1 (eBook)
https://doi.org/10.1007/978-3-031-99101-1

This Palgrave Macmillan imprint is published by the registered company Springer Nature Switzerland AG
The registered company address is: Gewerbestrasse 11, 6330 Cham, Switzerland

I believe in intuitions and inspirations. I sometimes feel that I am right. I do not know that I am.

—Albert Einstein

We write to taste life twice, in the moment and in retrospect.

—Anaïs Nin

Machines take me by surprise with great frequency.

—Alan Turing

I write to discover what I know.

—Flannery O'Connor

Acknowledgments

Sincere thanks go to the contributors, whose thoughts about *AI and Creative Writing* these are. Thanks also to colleagues at the Great Writing International Creative Writing Conference, which I direct. Your discussions, both formally in the conference sessions and informally outside of them, helped inspire progress on this book. The same goes for those from the UK, USA, China, Australia and Brazil who have joined me these past two years in video-linked discussions. Thanks to members of the Oakland University AI Taskforce, which I have co-chaired these past eighteen months with my colleague, the Dean of Engineering and Computer Science. Thanks to those attending the Institute on AI, Pedagogy, and the Curriculum at the American Association of Colleges and Universities (AAC&U). Webinars, discussions and mentoring at this AAC&U AI Institute have informed the work on this book. Further back, thanks to those at the Joint Information Systems Committee (JISC) the UK's not-for-profit organization that provides network and IT services and digital resources for further and higher education and research. Sitting as a creative writer on JISC committees for a few years in discussions around technology and research and technology and community development continues to inform how I think about technology in creative practice and technology in education. Without that JISC experience, it is unlikely this book would have happened. The same can be said for the influences of my time on the EU Commission's Panel of Experts at DG X (Information Communication Culture and Audiovisual Media) and as a panelist at the Arts and Humanities Research Council (AHRC). Combined, these two experiences emphasized the role creative practitioners can play in informing how we engage with technology, suggesting both possibilities and notes of caution. Thanks to Molly Beck at Palgrave Macmillan, who commissioned this book. Wonderful to work with you again, Molly! Thanks to Felicity, and to Shreenidhi and the team in Production. And, finally, thanks and love to my wife, Louise, for support on this writing project which travels into territory beyond the latest draft of a novel or a short story!

Contents

Introduction

Abstract To start: Ancient Greek myths; Jonathan Swift's word machine 'Engine' in *Gulliver's Travels*; Kapel Čapek's modernist play *R.U.R* and its robota—synthetic organic matter designed for work. Cinematic ziggurats, laboratories, and underground factories in Fritz Lang's *Metropolis*. Later films, such as *Star Wars* and *Short Circuit*. What it is to be human is core to the question of AI's relationship with creative writing, and we have explored this from the automatons of ancient Greek myths to contemporary literature and film. Attendant to that question is whether AI can have 'understanding', in our human sense. Creative writing provides a unique human space. A place where written language is used creatively, involving us combining our imaginations with forms of analysis. New knowledge emerges for creative writing—ideas, observations, and feelings are shared with the reader or audience. Can AI authentically occupy such a space? Is so, how, and to what ends? Can it assist creative writers? Can it hinder them? Machine learning pioneer, Alan Turing, once noted that at some point the teacher (in this case the creative writer) becomes unable to predict how the pupil (the artificial intelligence) will behave. That thought has fascinating implications for our sense of what creative writing is and why we humans do it. Here in this book, twelve interviewees—creative writers, technologists, and educators—consider ten questions about AI and creative writing. Their answers provide practical, historical, philosophical, technological, and artistic context and meaning.

G. Harper (ed.), *AI and Creative Writing*,
https://doi.org/10.1007/978-3-031-99101-1_1

Keywords Humanness · Alan Turing · Learning · Ancient · Perspective

I mostly introduce AI to audiences by mentioning its history, beginning with a brief reference to Ancient Greece, as does the American National Academy of Engineering (NAE), interestingly. You will also find AI tells its own story that way—because, of course, any Generative AI commonly used today draws on data it finds out in the digital world, and therefore, with a great deal of AI's history having some presence in the digital realm as news, articles and occasionally as books, the topics, themes and storylines AI incorporates into its story are also the ones I incorporate into the story I tell. Almost.

Almost, because AI is not a human being and I am. I have physically been to the ruins of the Acropolis of Athens and of the Temple of Olympian Zeus. I have joined the crowds lining up there. I have felt the cool Pentelic Marble of the temple known as the Erechtheum. I have hung out with Greek people—admittedly the modern not ancient kind—and shared meals with them. AI can't do any of that, and maybe we should consider if that really matters. Perhaps it doesn't. Afterall, AI draws on the work of humans anyway, right? In doing that, it is both what we have made it and what it simulates a human response to be, using amounts of data far exceeding those individual human beings are capable of accessing. As Ethan Mollick points out in *Co-Intelligence: Living and Working with AI* (2024), AI 'learns to recognize patterns, structures, and context in human language. Remarkably, with the vast number of adjustable parameters (called weights), [Large Language Models] LLMs can create a model that emulates how human communicate through written text' (Mollick 2024: 10).

Remarkably, indeed, because AI explores, determines the validity of what it finds, decides things, makes choices, and communicates. Through what is often referred to as 'connectionism', LLMs learn by coming to understand patterns in data. You can request something by prompting Generative AI, of which LLMs are a subset—that is, 'prompt it' by asking a Chatbot—and it will respond based on the data on which it has been trained. Prompt writing has therefore become an new and evolving writing skill. Prompts being essentially our instructions, of a certain, distinctive kind. But more than that. This is where AI (and LLMs in particular) becomes more than the outputs of the computer hardware and software with which most people have long been familiar. Much more, because AI acts and reacts as machinery that learns. Machine learning, this is, in the way described by computer scientist, philosopher, mathematical biologist and cryptanalyst Alan Turing in his famous paper 'Computing Machinery and Artificial Intelligence' (1950):

> An important feature of a learning machine is that its teacher will often be very largely ignorant of quite what is going on inside, although he may still be able to some extent to *predict* his pupil's behaviour. [my italics]. (Turing: 458)

'Predict', even today, because there is both a directional intention created by prompting the most common forms of AI and a human expectation that means behavioral iterations of responses by AI can be teased out with our interactive approaches. That said, what Turing referred to has also evolved to a greater degree of potential AI independence because, of course, the amount of data on which an LLM (for example) can be trained is so much vaster today than it was in Turing's time.

And yet, the human-AI relationship today echoes much of what Turing describes in his seminal 1950 paper (and I purposely use the word 'relationship' with the aim of later revisiting this word and concept). Prompt writing is perhaps our most notable example of how we use AI in iterative ways. With it, we aim to effectively converse with AI.

These conversations would hardly seem probable to many people—and certainly to relatively few people before the explosion of LLMs in the later part of 2022 (given much impetus by the launch of ChatGPT by the research organization OpenAI in November of that year). Very quickly a discussion of how to work with generative AI produced guidelines and books and further research and examples. The core of the actions we were undertaking related to the difference between AI and any knowledge of the digital world the general population had before AI became more commonplace. I return, briefly, in this, to Alan Turing and the 'learning machine' as he described and contemplated it. Turing's is a decisive consideration, not a mere categorization or an attempt to create a depiction of a type or style of computing. 'Learning' has a specific and yet also universal meaning for us, and it is to this that philosopher and biologist and computer scientist Turing is alluding.

We humans learn at various points in our lives and have gone so far as to define these points (mostly based on developmental stages in childhood), in socially and culturally determined ways, and in many parts of the world have developed highly structured and systematized approaches to individual and communal learning. We promote progress in learning and train people in modes of teaching that produce learning and use learning as a guide to understanding so much so that we have even colloquially suggested, with a sense of aspiration and openness to possibility, that anything can be learnt, if we each apply enough time and effort. Meaning, in this, that understanding and knowledge are available to us, if we make a commitment to learning.

Despite (or perhaps because of) the deep-rooted humanness in all this, we also tend to believe that animals can, indeed, learn, and that domestic animals (largely our pet dogs and cats) are well-suited to be our close companions because they are capable of being taught, and therefore of learning what they need to learn to successfully co-exist with us in our lives. We also believe that machines are capable of learning.

We believe today that machines are capable of learning, in the world at large, in work and in education for example, and in our personal lives. Learning is defined here as the ability to acquire knowledge and skills and certain behaviors. But, learning also suggests the acquisition of principles and of understanding and of perspectives. It is in our consideration of these aspects of learning that the question of the learning machine becomes most fraught. Can a machine understand? Can a machine develop principles? Can a machine have a perspective?

When thinking about creative writing, which is writing with the heightened contribution, stimulation and guidance of our individual human imaginations, one aspect that critics of AI find particularly challenging is that aspect we generally call 'understanding'. Certainly, generative AI can identify and analyze and interpret and chatbots built using Large Language Models (LLMs) can respond to human instructions as if they (colloquially speaking) 'understand' them. However, can they *actually* understand them?

Melanie Mitchell and David C. Krakauera in the *Proceedings of the National Academy of Science of the United States of America* comment:

> The debate over understanding in LLMs, as ever larger and seemingly more capable systems are developed, underscores the need for extending our sciences of intelligence in order to make sense of broader conceptions

of understanding for both humans and machines. (Mitchell and Krakauera 2023: 5)

So, when it comes to whether an AI can learn enough to understand we first need to determine what we mean by 'understanding'. LLMs are trained on large amounts of data, giving them the capacity to generate new data (new texts, when thinking about creative writing) based on what they have learned. With such large amounts of data many machine choices arise, so that using an LLM (and some of the first generally known AI chatbots, such as OpenAI's ChatGPT are notable here) can produce iterative results, one prompt producing one version, a further interaction refining that version, and so on and so on. Further still, multiple versions of any piece of creative writing become quickly available, iteration being not just possibly but often technically focal, when we are considering the AI's response, and new ideas can be applied by us to what could be said to be a conversation between human and machine. In some sense, the machine is comprehending. And it is highly likely that an AI's ability to find models on which to draw is far greater than our human capacity, given that the artificial neural networks it employs work with iterative processing algorithms to learn patterns, detect meta information and tags in the electronic world, and features in so much data so quickly that it exceeds our human ability to do this. And yet, understanding involves propositional conditions and causal concepts. Simply being able to find and discuss things does not constitute understanding. Nor does understanding only relate to relevance. It also relates to being able to determine situational, contextual or projected weight in an idea or observation or a discovery. In other words, understanding could be said to exceed the capabilities of AI to act and react fluidly, where judgment and value involves not only accumulation of information but projection of intent and meaning and even desire and satisfaction.

Similarly, when thinking about AI and creative writing, and indeed AI generally, the notion that learning involves principles and perspectives does not entirely negate a machine's potential learning, but questions do continue to abound.

In creative writing terms, principles and perspectives have long been fundamental both to the practice of writing creatively and to the reception of the works that creative writers produce. Principles in the sense of beliefs and ways of working, for example, so that creative writers create modes of undertaking their writing and incorporate beliefs—meta- notions, as it were—about their writing, into their acts and the results of doing the writing. Principles also in the sense of ethics, in that while it is not of course the case that creative writers are by definition always ethical, when we combine our imaginations and our intellects in order to write creatively we also delve into our individual psychology that informs that combining. There, quite naturally, we encounter principles—foundational aspects of our behavior. In that sense, Franziska Poszler, Edy Portmann and Christoph Lütge in an article in the journal *AI and Ethics*, have explored where principles in AI might be doable or even desirable. They write:

> To develop ethically grounded algorithms and technologies, scholars have suggested computational ethics as an essential frontier, which aims to translate ethical principles into computer code. However, computational ethics has received little attention in academic literature so far, with existing work mainly focusing on its technical implementation, while many open questions concerning its (societal and ethical) implications still need to be resolved. (Poszler et al. 2024)

Deciding if AI can have or should have principles in this computational ethics sense remains open to discussion.

Finally, to consider the notion of learning as something that incorporates perspective. Can a machine have a perspective? Creative writers are grounded in ideals of perspective, offering not only their personal attitudes, outlooks and viewpoints but also, frequently, being aware of how they might incorporate perspectives into their creative works, developing voice and tone and viewpoint in that respect. Additionally, a creative writer often considers what perspectives there might be among readers or audiences who receive their works—and how these might influence the communication between people that their written art brings about. Varieties of perspective define creative writing and works of creative writing. Can a machine learn to do this fundamental creative writing activity? Can it generally engage in learning if learning involves perspective?

Lacking self-awareness, it would seem impossible for AI to have perspective. Theoretically, however, Artificial General Intelligence [AGI] (which does not yet exist) could achieve something akin to perspective, along with a self-regulating sense of what perspectives entail, given that (theoretically) AGI would possess cognitive capabilities matching and then exceeding human capabilities. AGI could therefore have a high degree of autonomy and it could also accomplish metacognitive tasks, learning how it is learning and, in so doing, develop an understanding of perspectives, its own and others that exist beyond its own. And this self-understanding could generate a sense of machine identity, a distinguishing character to the AI you are using, which could include emulated memories, experiences and relationships, even though the AGI with which you are engaging would not be a human being.

But, for now (perhaps forever), can AI learn—if learning involves having understanding, and developing principles and having perspectives? Can it learn to truly write creatively, not merely emulate us writing creatively?

The jury is out.

Some things, however, are for certain: AI can indeed identify information, and it can analyze, and it can interpret. In doing so it can emulate human responses and develop this emulation in sophisticated ways so that, drawing on vast amounts of data available to it, it can (for example) produce stories and poems and scripts, among other creative things. We can prompt it to do this, and in the case of LLMs we can do that prompting in iterative ways, beginning either far from or close to an idea or thought or emotional context we wish to explore, and then proceeding to hone our communication with the AI so that what we produce by using this tool becomes the result of a kind of conversation between human and machine. We can adopt personas (that is, give our requests character and tone and voice) and in doing so encourage the AI to respond to the prompting personalities we create.

When using AI for creative writing purposes we can tell it (and I am largely talking, of course, chatbots built using LLMs) to respond in certain ways—to give attention to certain elements, highlight some things over others, adopt a tone, emulate a viewpoint, contrast or parallel or intersect aspects of showing or telling, of response to ideas or emotions, to draw on the data it can indeed draw upon in the electronic world and produce intersections with the nuances we ask it to adopt. But can it actually write creatively?

The jury is out.

The history of Artificial Intelligence is the history of our relationship with what we believe it means to be human. This relationship is both simple and complex, because we tend to believe we know the answer, but we don't tend to all agree entirely on every nuance, aspect and element. Humanness has been at the crux of our engagement with AI—how we determine the dimensions of that engagement and how we feel about it. The same goes for our consideration of AI and creative writing because in creative writing—in doing it and in the works we create by doing it—we see something exemplary about our human condition.

It is in creative writing that we take the ordinary, the everyday, the written word we might use formally or casually in other ways, and we make it remarkable. Perhaps in doing this we suggest other parts of the human experience are remarkable too. Perhaps, in using writing creatively we remind ourselves that the human imagination is as powerful as the human intellect, if not more so. Perhaps we empower ourselves to go beyond the day to day, while not letting go of the practical, the communicative, and the commonsensical. We instead give these things character and range and potential. For all these reasons, the history of our general relationship with AI is paralleled by how we think about AI and creative writing.

To explain the history of AI *The Bridge*, the journal of the American National Academy of Engineering (NAE), draws on the work of Adrienne Mayor in her book *Gods and Robots: Myths, Machines, and Ancient Dreams of Technology* (Mayor 2018). Mayor writes:

> the many visualizations of artificial life in the mythic writings were put to good use in antiquity, as provocative ways to think about alternative worlds, which in turn raised ethical and philosophical questions about agency and slavery. (154)

Mayor, a Stanford historian of ancient science and ancient wars, also notes in Chapter Seven of *Gods and Robots*, 'Hephaestrus: Divine Devices and Automata', that one of the 'one of the essential motivations for the creation of machines and robots is economic'. (Mayor, 152). Hephaestrus was the ancient Greek god of stonemasonry, metallurgy, blacksmithing, fire and, indeed, of machines.

The economic implications of our development of AI have certainly been in the foreground from the moment humans began considering it—not least in relation to and what Mayor refers to as 'slavery' (meaning machines relieving human workers from drudgery). Concerns about creative workers in the creative economy is one aspect of how we have been wary of AI development in relation to creative writing—posing for us such basic questions as whether there will be a role for creative writers in a world more influenced by AI and, if so, how this role might change as AI moves forward, potentially toward AGI. Creative writers have had these questions in mind themselves, and more generally in relation to the world around them.

The 1921 play *R.U.R*, an acronym for Rossumovi Univerzální Roboti (Rossum's Universal Robots) by Czech writer Karel Čapek, is based on a short story by Čapek and his brother Josef Čapek called 'The System', published in 1908. In R.U.R artificial humans (Robots) are organic beings, but cannot feel pain, have no emotions, and are designed for work—with the intention of relieving humankind from the drudgery of labor. 'Robot' is a translation of the Czech word 'robota', meaning 'forced labor' or 'slave'.

Before Čapek, Lemuel Gilliver in Jonathan Swift in *Gulliver's Travels* (1726), is introduced to 'the Engine', while visiting the Academy of Projectors in the land of Lagando. The depiction of the Engine here is reminiscent of our later fictional and factual depictions of computers and AI, as well as of how we humans might acquire and share knowledge. In the Academy of Projectors, Gulliver observes:

> The first professor I saw, was in a very large room, with forty pupils about him. After salutation, observing me to look earnestly upon a frame, which took up the greatest part of both the length and breadth of the room, he said, 'Perhaps I might wonder to see him employed in a project for improving speculative knowledge, by practical and mechanical operations.... Every one knew how laborious the usual method is of attaining to arts and sciences; whereas, by his contrivance, the most ignorant person, at a reasonable charge, and with a little bodily labour, might write books in philosophy, poetry, politics, laws, mathematics, and theology, without the least assistance from genius or study.' He then led me to the frame .... The professor then desired me 'to observe; for he was going to set his engine at work.' The pupils, at his command, took each of them hold of an iron handle .... (Swift, 176)

Using this engine, and 'with little bodily labor' a person 'might write books' of all kinds. *Gulliver's Travels* is Swift's most popular work. The engine he imagines requires 'the least assistance from genius or study' to enable people to write books. It is, in this way, 'economic' in a number of defined ways—creatively, durationally, as well as in the amount of labor and degree of skill and extent of human understanding required. Swift's 'engine' is also a prescient reference to the kinds of concerns that have abounded here, 300 years later, as the notion that it might indeed be figuratively just the pulling of an 'iron handle' that remains the role for a human writer in the age of Generative AI. Surely all else can now be handled by a machine?

When Fritz Lang released the science film *Metropolis*, in 1927, robotics (as well as the broader tenets of a silvery and socialized robotic AI) again were scrutinized, not only for the economic contributions such technologies might make but also for now they relate to what it means to be human. In this story, much like in *R.U.R*, the owners of industry and those who are workers in it are in conflict, and the role of what is effectively some kind of AI centers around the danger of ignoring core human values found in 'the heart' not only in 'the head'. Set in 2026 (ironically, we might say, given the timing of the wider emergence of Generative AI here in the twenty-first century), we meet in *Metropolis* the real and saintly Maria and her robotic double, Maria. Here the political and economic implications of what we can identify as AI confront the personal, generational implications as the workers' children are placed in physical danger. Making the right choice between real and the 'false' Maria is central to their survival. This crucial choice theme has been echoed by some of those fearful of AI today.

Fritz Lang's Maria returns fifty years later in the appearance and style of George Lucas's robot, C-3PO in *Star Wars* (1977), and in connected questions around AI, which continued well beyond the film franchise's original trilogy, and might continue yet in some form, into the future. C-3PO is a protocol android (a 'droid', as colloquially known). Fluent in over six million forms of communication—languages, in simple terms—C-3PO is designed to assist humans with cross-cultural etiquette and with multiple instances of translation. However, it is in C-3PO's relationship with the robotic R2D2, the astromech droid, starship mechanic and fighter pilot AI assistant that we encounter the most significant thinking around how humanness might or might not be present in AI.

C-3PO and R2D2 are, in every identifiably human sense, friends. Whether in a version of fantastical projection or of potential reality, they are two machines that are pleased to be with each other, talk with each other and care for each other. Both C-3PO and R2D2 show awareness and they show empathy—toward other robotic forms, towards humans, and in the bonds that are clear in their own relationship. Based on Akira Kurosawa's peasant farmers, Matashichi and Tahei, in his 1958 film *The Hidden Fortress* (Davies), the two droids provide comic relief, embody human traits in such things as worrying, stepping into harm's way while being aware that's what they are doing, and in contemplating their own actions. With C-3PO's language capabilities we also find this Maria-like droid interpreting the smaller robot's whistling and beeping, so that characters within the film's world and audiences peering into it find themselves invited into a seemingly 'live' AI condition in which failure to understand, learn or emote is not based in the faults of the machines but, rather, in the inadequacies of those who encounter them.

By the time Mercedes-Benz was trialing their first driverless vehicles in the streets around Bundeswehr University Munich in the mid-1980s, including one well-known instance of a driverless Benz reaching speeds of up to 185 km/h (115 mph) on the autobahn, the *Star Wars* film franchise had spawned theme parks, animated TV series and TV 'holiday specials'. More importantly for our thinking about AI and creative writing, the notion of a world in which humans and machines might not share the same status but do in some way and by some means project something of the same ideals and outlooks was becoming commonplace—and the popular cinematic world reflected this.

A relatively contemporary concept of the human-machine relationship emerged in such popular 1980s Hollywood films as *War Games* (1983) and its war simulation program 'Joshua', named after its creator's deceased son, and *The Terminator* (1984), which quickly became the foremost filmic reference point for hostile AI. It was seen too in *Short Circuit* (1986), in which one of a number of robots designated as S.A.I.N.T. (Strategic Artificially Intelligent Nuclear Transport), malfunctions after being struck by lightning arcing its electrical circuitry and power bus, and afterward claims it is alive. A Frankensteinian reference perhaps. 'Number 5 is alive!' it repeats, with increasing urgency, racing away from its potential captors (human beings representing both unchecked governmental officialdom and a general lack of compassion). Much of the rest of the film involves sympathetic human characters trying to ensure this 'living' AI, this threatened robot 'survives'.

Those 1980s film years were, of course, already into the era of the Apple II home computer, which introduced home computing to a great many people, and was also launched in the *Star Wars* year of 1977, incidentally, and manufactured through into the early 1990s—being joined along the way by PCs and the reach of the Microsoft Corporation, which dominated personal computing in that period. providing an increasingly commonplace sense of computing in every home and, as with much of the contemporary population in much of the world, creative writers were increasingly familiar (and often comfortable) with such things spelling and grammar checks and certainly by the dawn of the twenty-first century 1990s with the ability to seek out and apply information found on the World Wide Web.

Alan Turing's work and the 1956 summer research project at Dartmouth College, where the term 'artificial intelligence' was first used, were long past when the AI-informed films *Lost in Space* and *The Matrix* were screened in the later years of the twentieth century.

In 2001, George Lucas's friend and sometime collaborator, Steven Spielberg, released his film, *A.I. Artificial Intelligence*, in which David, a robotic boy, is programmed to love, but suffers the shock of finding out that he is not as individual as he thinks he is. Rather, he is one of many similar 'David' Mecha (a new type of robot) and, Pinocchio-like, he can only seek out humanness not, by default, possess it.

The automatons imagined in Ancient Greece, the engine in *Gulliver's Travels*, the *robota* of Capek's *R.U.R.*, James Cameron's *Terminator* and David and the other Mecha of *AI Artificial Intelligence* all offer popular cultural creative responses to what was happening in the world around them, from the ancient and mythical machines of Hephaestrus, to the steam engines, and spinning jennies and metallurgy of eighteenth century Britain, to the inventions and industrial expansion at the opening of the twentieth century, the arrival of the automobile and the airplane, the increasing success of the telephone, to the post-WWII period of Cold War scientific revolution of the mid-twentieth century, which included the 1947 invention of the transistor, the extensions and leaps made during the Space Race (from solar cells to LEDs to laptops), to the digitally fueled expansions of domestic and commercial computing in the later twentieth century and the emergence of smart phone technologies and domestic virtual reality technologies. By 2010 Apple had introduced digital assistant Siri, developed by the Stanford Research Institute International Artificial Intelligence Center; and, in 2014, Amazon's measured female voiced assistant Alexa soon began appearing on kitchen benches and side tables in much of the industrialized world. 'I'm sorry, I didn't quite get that,' became a common conversation rejoinder—between human and machine, that is (or, perhaps, machine imitation approached domestic caricature!).

We have, in all these ways, domesticated many of the technologies around us, and in doing so often considered notions of what is 'artificial' intelligence and what is 'human' in our humanness to the extent that to suggest somehow, a few decades into the twenty-first century, we were surprised by the rise of Generative AI and what it might mean to such human pursuits as creative writing is patently (if artlessly) false. We have long been aware of the opportunities, the threats, the innocuities, the information and misinformation, the capabilities, the inabilities, the reasoning and the irrationality that over time has surrounded our invention and interaction with machine technologies.

1 This Book

The contributors to this book include creative writers, engineers, technologists and educationalists. My approach was to ask them 10 questions connected with our response to, interest in, potential use of and expanding sense of AI. The focus was to be AI in relation to creative writing, and on the AI we see expanding in the twenty-first century with a focus on Generative AI and the kinds of natural language processing is most impacting our thoughts on how AI impacts creative writing. The aim was not to consider specific AI platforms, certain AI programs, or particular AI products or services; but, rather, to look more deeply into how we feel about, and think about AI in relation to creative writing and to approach that relationship from these multiple perspectives. Each contributor answered the questions posed in the way they chose to answer them—no additional monitoring or shaping of answers was imposed. The questions asked are these:

1. When someone says 'Artificial Intelligence' what things do you think about?
2. Thinking of antonyms of 'intelligence', would it be possible, do you think, to have 'Artificial Unintelligence' or 'Artificial Stupidity' or 'Artificial Awkwardness' and, if so, what might they look like?
3. What kinds of things can AI help creative writers do? What kind of AI might help them best?
4. What things can AI not help creative writers do? (and this could be specifically associated with their writing or more generally in their lives)
5. If you knew a novel, or a poem or a screenplay was written using AI would it make any difference to how you responded to it as a reader or audience? Does the form of writing make any difference to your response—so, for example, if you knew a film you

were watching had a script written using AI or, alternatively, if you were reading a novel written using AI? Does genre make any difference—for example, if you were reading a sonnet or an elegy, or if you were reading a science fiction short story, or if you were reading a video game script for an adventure game?

6. Does any AI have imagination? If so, in way or ways? It not, why not? Do you believe it could ever have imagination?
7. The previous question touched on the notion of whether AI can itself be imaginative. The follow up, then, is whether it can (itself) form new ideas, have sensations, form memories? Can AI actually think? Can it feel?
8. It might have been impossible for someone from the medieval period, where the quill was the primary writing tool and parchment the medium, to imagine a world in which word processors existed. Speculating as much as you like, what do you imagine the writing world will look like in 20 years, 50 years, and 200 years?
9. If you had all the time you needed, what written work would you like to write and why? It doesn't have to be a work of creative writing. Would you use AI to write it; and, if so, how would you use it?
10. Who benefits most from using AI? Anyone more than anyone else? Any industry more than any other industry? Any place or places in the world? Do you think more people or fewer people might write creatively because of the existence and application of AI—if so, why; if not, why not?

With creative writing as the focus, human creativity, economics, our well-being, decision-making, the nature of human knowledge, the potential, power and role of the human imagination, communication between human beings, the productive use of tools, our desires and satisfactions. These, among other topics, are all broached here in relation to *AI and Creative Writing*.

Graeme Harper

References

Davies, Brett, Droids and Peasants: Akira Kurosawa's Thematic Influence on the Star Wars Saga. In *The Kyoto Conference on Arts, Media & Culture 2021, Official Conference Proceedings*, https://papers.iafor.org/wp-content/uploads/papers/kamc2021/KAMC2021_60706.pdf. Last accessed November 3, 2024.

Mayor, Adrienne. 2018. *Gods and Robots: Myths, Machines and Ancient Dreams of Technology*. Princeton: Princeton University Press.

Mitchell, Melanie, and David C. Krakauera. 2023. The Debate over Understanding in AI's Large Language Models. *Proceedings of the National Academy of Science of the United States of America* (PNAS) 120 (13, March 28). https://www.pnas.org/toc/pnas/120/13. Last accessed October 25, 2024.

Mollick, Ethan. 2024. *Co-Intelligence: Living and Working with AI*. Portfolio: New York.

National Academy of Engineering. 2021. From Ancient Greeks to Self-Driving Cars and Beyond.. https://www.nae.edu/244888/Artificial-Intelligence-From-Ancient-Greeks-to-SelfDriving-Cars-and-Beyond. Last accessed October 27, 2024.

Poszler, F., E. Portmann, and C. Lütge. 2024. Formalizing Ethical Principles Within AI Systems: Experts' Opinions on Why (Not) and How to Do It. *AI Ethics*. https://doi.org/10.1007/s43681-024-00425-6. Last accessed October 25, 2024.

Swift, Jonathan. 1998. *Gulliver's Travels*. Oxford: Oxford University Press.

Turing, A. M. 1950. Computing Machinery and Intelligence. *Mind: A Quarterly Review of Psychology and Philosophy* LIX (236, October).

Shady Cosgrove

Abstract **Shady Cosgrove** says: AI's capacity to learn, without embodied experience, complicates our sense of it. It does so because it challenges our traditional ideas of knowledge, of creativity, and of the human subject. Philosophical, pedagogical, and emotional concerns arise. While AI can support creative writers, perhaps helping to overcome writer's block, or assisting with revisions, AI can't possess an imagination, or have true understanding or perspective, in our human sense. And the irrationality, urgency, and emotional resonance that drive human creativity are absent. Literary theory, Australian Indigenous knowledge and educational practice assist us in understanding AI's potential relationships with creative writing, but the lack of embodiment and experiential memory precludes empathy and raises questions about intention (or the lack of intention) in AI. Creative writing is ultimately rooted in lived human experience, vulnerability, and imaginative risk—none of which AI can possess. There are also concerns about the environmental impact of AI and about socio-economic impact (concerns raised vividly in the 2023 Writers Guild of America strike). The future will depend not solely on technological advancement but on how humans choose to engage with and shape technological tools.

Keywords Mimesis · Rewriting · Empathy · Genre · Industries

G. Harper (ed.), *AI and Creative Writing*,
https://doi.org/10.1007/978-3-031-99101-1_2

Shady Cosgrove Writes on Dharawal land and teaches creative writing at the University of Wollongong in Australia. Her research interests include prose fiction, prose poetry, microfiction, embodied creative practice, narratology and pedagogy. Her most recent book *Flight* (Gazebo Books) is a collection of prose poetry, exploring the linked tensions of flight and longing, and her other books include *What the Ground Can't Hold* (Picador) and *She Played Elvis* (Allen and Unwin). Her short works and articles have appeared in *Best Australian Stories, Anthology of Australian Prose Poetry, Dreaming Awake, New Writing, TEXT, Animal Studies Journal, The Writing Mind, The Incompleteness Books I and II, Cordite, Overland, Antipodes, Southerly, Island, takahe, Eunoia Review*, and various Spineless Wonders collections. She has judged the Joanne Burns Award and received an Australian National University Humanities Research Centre Fellowship, a Bundanon Artists Residency, the Varuna House Eleanor Dark Flagship Fellowship and a Nan Tien Temple and South Coast Writers Center residency. For more information, see www.shadycosgrove.com.

1. When someone says 'Artificial Intelligence' what things do you think about?

'To qualify as AI, a system must exhibit some level of learning and adapting' (Siemens 2022). It is this notion of an entity learning and adapting, without consciousness, that compels me: maybe because it upsets notions of the humanist liberal subject. This is not a bad thing. I am trying to unlearn my own anthropocentrism as I consider Australian Indigenous notions of Country and how they question the Western premise of the centralized human animal, and maybe there's a well-placed irony to the fact AI also makes me question these assumptions. Maybe because I teach, because I think so much about my students—as human subjects, individuals—and how they learn. Learning traditionally has been connected to notions of experience. The Oxford English Dictionary (2024) defines learning as, 'To acquire knowledge of (a subject) or skill in (an art, etc.) as a result of study, experience, or teaching'. AI acquires information, but is that knowledge? AI learning does not result in knowledge from 'study, experience, or teaching'. If AI can learn without experiencing, it complicates notions of learning and enforces a re-evaluation of how we consider—and what language we use to discuss—the sharing/transferring of information and knowledge. And can 'knowledge' be transferred?—the OED defines 'knowledge' as 'familiarity gained by experience', something that invokes epistemology and the subjective.

I asked ChatGPT for a (textual) AI creative self-portrait, and it responded with: 'This self-portrait is not static but dynamic, ever-evolving as I learn and grow with each interaction. It embodies the essence of what it means to be an AI: a blend of technology and human-like understanding, always learning, always adapting' (ChatGPT, accessed on July 31, 2024). It is this insistence on 'learning' and the 'like' in 'human-like' that forces my consideration, reminding me of James Phelan, discussing fictional characters.

> Silently underlying this discussion of the mimetic component (of the fictional character) are some messy problems. First, all this talk about characters as plausible or possible persons presupposes that we know what a person is. But the nature of the human subject is of course a highly contested issue among contemporary thinkers. (Phelan 1989: 11)

One could substitute 'AI' for 'fictional character' in this above passage and in so doing perhaps get at something deeper: just as fictional characters force us to reckon with what it means to be human, so too does AI. In considering what it is and how it relates to the human, we are forced to reckon with what it means to be human, and this—as Phelan points out—is highly contested terrain.

2. Thinking of antonyms of 'intelligence', would it be possible, do you think, to have 'Artificial Unintelligence' or 'Artificial Stupidity' or 'Artificial Awkwardness' and, if so, what might they look like?

While AI has been improving with mathematical calculations, recent iterations have been better at navigating the liberal arts (Lohr 2024) because AI 'are fine-tuned for determining probabilities, not doing rules-based calculations … Traditionally, computers have been programmed to follow step-by-step rules and retrieve information in structured databases' (Lohr 2024). More than a decade ago AI designers shifted approach, programming AI as: 'a neural network loosely modeled on the human brain' (Lohr 2024). This shift toward general intelligence is more far-reaching, aiming to 'adequately model the world with all the entirety of knowledge, in a consistent and useful manner' (Siemens 2022). AI is improving with mathematical calculations but this point in its development is key to the current negotiation between the human animal subject and AI because of its focus on mimesis—mimesis was programmed into AI. The idea of an AI demonstrating artificial awkwardness, an attribute that seems remarkably human and yet something humans generally try to avoid, gets at something related to my uneasiness with AI. Of course, I can imagine an AI designed to simulate awkwardness, but AI doesn't feel, it cannot understand the sensation of feeling awkward. To draw on my answer above, awkwardness is important because it is an experience/emotion that teaches: it teaches human animals about social nuance and interaction. This seems to underline a key way that AI *cannot* learn. It cannot learn through experiencing feelings. It can learn by amassing data about reactions, outcomes and situations, but not from *feeling*. In thinking about this, I wonder: why am I attached to the idea that feeling is important, that feeling awkward is important in the terrain of human experience? Is it because I want to reiterate the primacy of the human animal experience (both the human animal and the concept of 'experience')? Maybe this gets at something American thinker Evan Darwin Winet means when he says, 'Why can't we just see AI as a tool? An "artifice" (like a toaster or your smart phone) that is prosthetic, extending and augmenting, rather than replacing, human functions. Is it because we fear AI will be autonomous? Functioning independently and without us? Actually REPLACING us?'.

3. What kinds of things can AI help creative writers do? What kind of AI might help them best?

As someone who struggles with first drafts and prefers revision, I can understand the desire to use AI to avoid the blank page. That is, enter the required parameters, and use AI (whether it proves proficient or not) to give the writer something to revise. Even if the draft is incompetent, it can offer a starting point or a continuation when the author is stuck. For instance, SudoWrite, a subscription AI, 'provides capabilities such as continuing a story where you left off, describing a scene, rewriting according to some guidelines, brainstorming plot points, and feedback' (Gero et al. 2023: 3). While I have experimented with AI prompts, I worry entrusting AI to deliver a first draft—even if radically re-visioned by the author a la Ship of Theseus—would give AI the power of first iteration and in so doing prioritize programming bias. As unidentified writer W1 in the study 'Social Dynamics of AI Support in Creative Writing' commented, 'once something is on the page it becomes just a bit harder to imagine what else it can be' (Gero et al. 2023: 9). Also, it is often in my first drafts (sprawling and uncomfortable, with huge tracts of unusable text) when themes emerge, and it is the very discomfort of facing the blank page that triggers the deep work required for writing. That is, AI may alleviate discomfort, but this may ultimately be unhelpful, if not obstructive, to the creative process. As a student articulated in my 'Creative Writing Major Project' class last week: 'Yes, sitting down is difficult, but it's necessary, and my love for writing outweighs that difficulty' (Dinning 2024).

AI can also help writers interrogate their work, and I would use AI for draft feedback if I did not have a community of writers to draw upon, especially if a work had personal themes that I was not ready to share with an audience. Though, it is important to remember that AI cannot understand the author's perspective when offering feedback. As writer W1 states, 'it's not like the computer can understand what you want to say; they can only see what you have written' (Gero et al. 2023: 5). Having said that, I would use AI to test drafts, as per unidentified writer W4.

> W4, a TV comedy writer ... discussed the difficulty of writing humorous scenes when people have seen so much TV already. She imagined using a computer to push herself and her writing further, saying, 'I might take a first stab at a scene, then I would give the computer the first bit and be like 'you write it'. And then if I wrote the same thing as the computer, I'd know I have to do better'. She explained further, 'I feel like comedy rests on surprise. So I wouldn't trust a computer to do that. Or if the computer did do that, then there has to be something better'. (Gero et al. 2023: 10)

AI can also prove useful with secondary research, especially for authors tracking description and location detail when primary research is not possible. Of course this can be risky—as writer Barbara Kingsolver reminds us, 'The difference between amateur and professional research is a willingness to back away from other people's accounts of what is, and find your own. There is no "googlesmell"' (Kingsolver 2014: 1). AI is like accessing a database of other people's accounts, based on luck of the logarithm. Kingsolver says:

> If I want to remove you from your life and whisk you into a picnic on the banks of a river in Teotihuacán, here are some things I need to know: what grows there, what trees, what flowers, in that month of the year? What does it smell like, are there bees? …

While Kingsolver worries that someone else's account of these kinds of details would 'likely render a flat, one-dimensional scene' sometimes authors are bound by external constraints (caring responsibilities or socio-economic/location/temporal/physical constraints), and cannot travel for research. It is true that experiencing something directly can enable a richer understanding, especially when we consider the importance of point-of-view and the *way* focalization operates to give readers information via the lens of character and voice. But as is often the case with AI, while there may be more desirable methods, it can help writers amass information—for instance, the names of trees, flowers, when they are in bloom, etc.—though at this stage fact-checking is still required. AI can also provide an ease for navigating and incorporating information that Google and Wikipedia lack.

4. What things can AI not help creative writers do? (and this could be specifically associated with their writing or more generally in their lives)

Sonic branding agency Stephen Arnold Music and sonic testing agency SoundOut undertook a study to test the empathetic appeal of AI-generated music. The study tested four kinds of compositions: 'AI-generated, AI supplemented by human modification, human generated, and human supplemented by AI modification' and found that 'human compositions outperform AI-generated material both in terms of overall appeal and accuracy when it comes to evoking specific emotions' (Taylor 2024). However, as David Courtier-Dutton, Founder of SoundOut, commented:

> While humans still outperform AI on the emotional front, the study has revealed that AI 'composing by numbers' is already not far behind. The AI was not bad, it was just not as good. The 2023 argument that AI cannot be creative has all but been settled, this study demonstrates that AI can also compose music to move us emotionally, it now just needs a little more technical empathy. (Reported in Taylor 2024)

Of course, this argument depends on how one defines 'creativity', a topic that has occupied critical thinkers for decades (Kris 1952; Campbell 1960; Maslow 1967; Csikszentmihalyi 1988; Dollinger et al. 2004; Jones et al. 2016) and the notion of 'technical empathy' seems telling here. Can we be 'technically empathetic'? AI does not compose music nor write literature because it is inspired by an irrational desire to write, it does not write from a position of urgency or awkwardness (as discussed above). Screenwriter Simon Rich (2023) states:

> I know that AIs will read [this article] closely, to scrape its data, and when they do, I hope they realize something: they will never stop me from writing ... If there's one edge I have over AI, it's this irrationality, this need to create something that has no right or reason to exist. I know it makes no sense. I'm starting to think it might also be what makes me human.

I question Rich's use of the verb 'realize'—does AI 'realize' or will it simply log information—but Rich's point remains: AI creates content because it has been directed to. I cannot help but think the circumstances of production (that is, operating from a desire/desperation to create) affect the objects of production. By producing text, AI does not alleviate the writer from the need to create. It may affect the writer's place in consumer markets (and this has very real socio-economic ramifications for writers) but even this I question. AI will continue adapting and perfecting formula-based outputs, but work that engages with the irrational and unpredictable aspects of the human condition will be difficult to mimic. I am aware this risks a certain romanticism, but the role of embodiment seems critical. When we speak of the human condition, part of this is the knowledge that we are corporeal: we grow older and die. AI can be programmed to mimic this, but AI cannot 'feel', 'live', or 'die'. Unidentified writer S19 noted that a computer does not bring the same kind of intention that another person does. 'Obviously, you have a reason why you are writing a story. And I think that is something [AI programming system] SudoWrite can't reproduce' (Gero et al. 2023: 9).

Too, writers bring perception of detail to their writing, a point-of-view that cannot be replicated (it can be copied, but only after the fact of creation). Writers bring complicated understandings of what it means to be human and alive. Again, this argument risks sounding like the liberal human subject will prove creative savior, however the fact remains that AI depends on human output to sustain productivity—it is not independent. And provided writers find new and innovative ways to describe the world, they will be irreplaceable. In *How Proust Can Change Your Life*, Alain de Botton states,

> …we see the pyramids at Giza and go, 'That's nice'. This (comment) is asked to account for an experience, but (its) poverty prevents either ourselves or our interlocutors from really understanding what we have lived through. We stay on the outside of our impressions, as if staring at them through a frosted window, superficially related to them, yet estranged from whatever has eluded causal definition. (p. 87)

AI is giving writers an opportunity to make themselves essential, but in order to do that we have to break windows and get inside of our impressions. We can't rely on the vague or the nice. As Winet (2024) states:

> And so the call for human writers to be bold in the tradition of Proust. To feel and experience deeply, and to lean in to our ignorance and awkwardness. To be vulnerable in a way that AI, by its nature, cannot be.

It is worth noting here that in a study by management academic Anil R Doshi and economist Oliver Houser, AI was found to be more useful for less experienced and creative writers:

> Access to GenAI ideas causes an increase in the writer's creativity with stories being evaluated as better written and more enjoyable, especially among less creative writers. However, GenAI-enabled stories are more similar to each other than stories by humans alone. (2023: abstract)

That is, GenAI can help even out the talent field, but it tends toward the repetitive, and highly talented writers find AI less useful.

5. If you knew a novel, or a poem or a screenplay was written using AI would it make any difference to how you responded to it as a reader or audience? Does the form of writing make any difference to your response—so, for example, if you knew a film you were watching had a script written using AI or, alternatively, if you were

reading a novel written using AI? Does genre make any difference—for example, if you were reading a sonnet or an elegy, or if you were reading a science fiction short story, or if you were reading a video game script for an adventure game?

Millicent Weber, an academic at the Australian National University, argues that readers like to connect with story and authors are part of the promotional machines used to sell books (2023). In an interesting twist, this means the human author is both author and paratext, and this position of author-as-paratext provides the reader with a way to frame the text as a human-crafted artifact, which may prove important in salvaging the place of the writer within commodified structures. Researcher and consultants Keith Kirkpatrick and Roger Firestein agree there is something in this notion of 'personhood':

> For the consumers of art, poetry, literature, music, or other creative content, enjoyment is often derived from the authentic, shared human experiences that are referenced to create that art. 'It's in the person', Firestien [of the Center for Applied Imagination at the State University of New York College at Buffalo] says. 'Can a computer fall in love? No. Can a computer be depressed? No. Can a computer go through the pandemic? No'.

If we read to connect with an author, it affects the reading experience to know a text did not originate with another person. Having said that, sometimes ChatGPT does a better job than human writers. Frustrated with the number of fantasy dragon stories my students were submitting (that relied on the fact of dragons to create reader interest), I entered the terms 'dragon' and 'mourning' into ChatGPT. AI offered a story about a dragon whose friends and family had all been murdered by humans so our protagonist dragon went to the far side of the mountain to commit suicide. While it was bleak, I admit the story felt more interesting than many of the assessments I've marked on the topic of dragons. Maybe this was because the AI did not rely on genre tropes nor the signifier of dragon (or what they have meant in other texts) to carry reader interest: the AI used larger story structures (catalyst, action, and reaction) to drive the narrative and the dragon was treated as a character. My point here being that while AI may write from an accumulation of data—so, too, can humans, and AI has much larger stores of information to draw upon. As Gero et al. state: '[AI program] SudoWrite is more general, but also more well-read and capable' (2023: 8). And sometimes a certain authorial detachment may be preferable because it can save the text from falling into cliché.

The issue of genre is key—readers and writers bring different expectations to different genres. I think here of a fantasy novel versus a prose poem, and am tempted to assert that plot may be easier to program than epiphany or character, however, components of narrative and poetics are not so easy to compartmentalize. Nineteenth century writer Henry James asked (1884): 'What is character but the determination of incident? What is incident but the illustration of character?' Of course, structuralists argued against the primacy of character (Barthes 1970) and yet the point remains that plot and character are enmeshed. Plot can operate as a way of 'showing' character, which is linked to voice and point-of-view. Plot is also linked to structure (the ordering of event) which is connected with how temporality is managed within a text. So while AI may be able to 'make things happen' at key points in a text, and in the microfiction context where there is less opportunity for nuance, I am less certain about longer works where there is more scope for multi-layered readings.

6. Does any AI have imagination? If so, in way or ways? It not, why not? Do you believe it could ever have imagination?

How can AI have imagination when it is dependent on sourcing data that already exists? This is not to say that AI does not have the capacity to be creative (complicated though that term may be). As was reported in *Scientific Reports* journal (Hubert et al. 2024), GPT-4 actually scored higher than human test participants for divergent thinking, a key component in assessing creativity:

> Overall, GPT-4 was more original and elaborate than humans on each of the divergent thinking tasks, even when controlling for fluency of responses. In other words, GPT-4 demonstrated higher creative potential across an entire battery of divergent thinking tasks (i.e., Alternative Uses Task, Consequences Task, and Divergent Associations Task).

At present, AI is successful across an array of divergent thinking exercises. However, it siphons data that already exists—it is not creating data in its own right. In order to stay relevant, AI needs contemporary data to be effective, but 'widespread data restrictions may pose a threat to A.I companies, which need a steady supply of high-quality data to keep their models fresh and up-to-date' (Roose 2024). Imagination and creativity are often connected to notions of the new and the innovative. Having an imagination links with knowing, learning, perceiving and realizing: verbs that are human-centric and experience-based, experiences that are attached to the corporeal. While AI can exist in body-form, that is different from living and feeling with the physical limitations and frailties that accompany the human embodied experience. AI doesn't have that ingenuity, but it does have access to multitudes of data and information—far more than a human could ever read and process. Writer S20 describes the differences between human and AI feedback (Gero et al. 2023: 8):

> A peer is someone who is grounded in a very specific point of view, and culture and identity and preference ... when I turn to SudoWrite, I know that I'm getting feedback and interactions with my work that is not personal at all . . . The amount of information on hand that SudoWrite is pulling from is this vast trove. And that's something that a human could never, even if they're well read, could really never achieve.

7. The previous question touched on the notion of whether AI can itself be imaginative. The follow up, then, is whether it can (itself) form new ideas, have sensations, form memories? Can AI actually think? Can it feel?

No—but does that matter? Can I be certain my friends and loved ones are thinking and feeling? I am bound by my consciousness. One of the reasons I love reading is because it offers an illusion of occupying another consciousness. Alan Palmer draws on Georges Poulet in 'The Construction of Fictional Minds' (2002: 30):

> Because of the strange invasion of my person by the thoughts of another, I am a self who is granted the experience of thinking thoughts foreign to him. I am the subject of thoughts other than my own. My consciousness behaves as though it were the consciousness of another. (Poulet 1969: 56)

When we read we don't literally become the characters we imagine, but we are given access to an imagined construction of another perspective. If AI is convincing enough, it may offer illusions of thinking and feeling that prove difficult to discern from human consciousness. In the same way that we suspend disbelief when we read a novel, we can suspend disbelief regarding the subjectivity of AI. And if I am not told an entity is operating with AI, how would I know? Children can imagine entire worlds and personalities for inanimate objects (as a four-year-old I spent days absorbed under the Christmas tree, mapping out the complex social dynamics and power hierarchies of the ornaments, or think of a child's favorite stuffed animal, lost just before bedtime, or the emotive power of *The Velveteen Rabbit*). Regardless of whether AI can actually think and imagine, humans may decide to treat it as if it can. I am thinking now of Kazuo Ishiguro's *Klara and the Sun* (2021) where the AI represented was more empathetic and thoughtful than its/her human counterparts. Is there a difference in humanizing a fictional (human) character and a fictional (AI) character?

Is the mimetic anxiety regarding AI related to not-knowing if it is being employed? Or the worry that AI could be more convincingly human than humans? Is this worry about control? Or is it about border anxiety? The need to keep humans and machines/tools separate? Or is it about notions of 'authenticity' and 'realness': is AI potentially problematic because an inert object can pretend to think and learn and create? There seems to be a media anxiety that the liberal subject will be replaced, but perhaps it is more useful to think about AI as offering complementary skillsets. AI may be a tool at the behest of the human subject, but the human subject is also shaped by its relationship with tools. Hammers aren't necessarily murderous weapons, though they can be. They can also be used to construct houses and places of safety. Maybe AI is confronting because the non-human AI writer *can* affect the human subject reader and thus be accorded a human-like respect. That is, the machine is more than a tool: while it can be manipulated, it can also manipulate—something that could trouble the primacy of the human liberal subject.

8. It might have been impossible for someone from the medieval period, where the quill was the primary writing tool and parchment the medium, to imagine a world in which word processors existed. Speculating as much as you like, what do you imagine the writing world will look like in 20 years, 50 years, and 200 years?

I wonder if writing and book-length works will even exist—not because of AI, but because of an over-reliance on screen use. Attention spans and the ability to focus for extended periods of time are already being impacted. Dr Liraz Margalit argues we need to curb screen time in young children because it affects the ability to focus, concentrate and communicate with other people (2016) and she is not alone (see Muppalla et al. 2023; Webster et al. 2019; Twenge et al. 2018). Our writing is in the process of becoming entertainment that cannot sit still. Of course, there are exceptions. I think here of Wim Wenders' *Perfect Days* as a creative work that operates in antithesis to this trend of relentless and busy entertainment.

I asked ChatGPT what creative writing would be like in twenty, fifty and two-hundred years, and it offered the same answer for all three time spans. This vagueness seems to epitomize the tensions of AI in its current form. It provided a sensible (though market-based) answer, saying there will probably be new storytelling formats, specifically in the form of more interactive experiences, as well as platforms to cater for more 'diverse voices … hybrid genres … eco-literature … global collaborations … microfiction and flash fiction … [and] AI co-creation'. However, it was unable to tease out the differences between various periods of time. AI can offer interesting starting points (I admit I liked ChatGPT's focus on diversity and environment issues, as well as microfiction and flash fiction) but it is not currently advanced enough to do the work of deeper critical or imaginative engagement.

9. If you had all the time you needed, what written work would you like to write and why? It doesn't have to be a work of creative writing. Would you use AI to write it; and, if so, how would you use it?

I don't know if I write with a written work in mind or if I write because I operate with Simon Rich's irrationality regarding the creative (cited above). That is, I write as a way to more deeply engage with a human condition that is, for me at present, connected with Australian Indigenous knowledges relating to kinship and Country. Even if I am not exploring my autobiographical experiences, writing provides a site where I can explore ideas-thoughts-feelings via language (sometimes propelled by story and event, sometimes inspired by metaphor or revelation). Because writing in this way is not about output—it's about the creative, dialogic impulse—I don't know that I am driven by the idea of finishing one written work. Writing has become less about outcome for me, and more a means for exploration and figuring. As poet Paul Hetherington (2022) writes, 'Although I strive hard to "finish" the prose poems I publish and, as it were, put them finally to bed, sometimes one will return like an insistent haunting, asking for renewed attention' (99). When he returns to the prose poem, it is not with the desire to improve it. Instead, it is as if 'the work is saying, "I contain something else that you are yet to write"' (99).

Despite this emphasis on process, I am working on many projects, and it would be nice to see some of them emerge into the world: a collaborative book about how Country can teach us about Story and Story can help us care for Country, a series of short-short prose poems and microfictions about Australia, a novel about couple-swapping and negotiating the domestic, a series of fragments about the role of the object in late capitalism, a collection of prose poems inspired by metaphor and love/the domestic. I don't see myself using AI with these projects, though I can see it being useful in the revising/editing stages as per comedic writer N4 cited up above, who uses AI to test whether ideas are overused/cliche. I am also inspired by Wim Wenders' *Perfect Days*, and would like to write something that affects readers in the way that movie affected me—that is, something that draws attention to the very act of living as meditation. I do not look at trees or wash the dishes in the same way after watching that film.

10. Who benefits most from using AI? Anyone more than anyone else? Any industry more than any other industry? Any place or places in the world? Do you think more people or fewer people might write creatively because of the existence and application of AI—if so, why; if not, why not?

My first thought is the electricity industry may be the one to benefit most from AI. As reported in *Scientific American* (Leffer 2023):

> A continuation of the current trends in AI capacity and adoption are set to lead to NVIDIA shipping 1.5 million AI server units per year by 2027. These 1.5 million servers, running at full capacity, would consume at least 85.4 terawatt-hours of electricity annually—more than what many small countries use in a year, according to the new assessment.

This will obviously have a large environmental impact, even with an increased focus on renewable energies. It also matters who owns and develops AI systems because that will impact invisible restrictions in place around issues of programming and data management. Like the means of production, those who understand and control AI will be able to use it for their ends. As well, because AI is computer-bound, there is a certain socio-economic privilege required for its access that supports the power/privilege structures that have made its creation possible. Though I like to think there is subversive potential to AI—either in folks hacking into systems or the systems themselves creating unexpected ways of engaging with information—that remains to be seen. However AI has already shown its broad-reaching impact on our creative industries—the 2023 Writers Guild of America strikes demonstrated the potential threat of AI to writers' jobs, especially the fear that movie production houses and corporations would prioritize finance over quality, and use AI to cut writing costs. As Raphael Bob-Waksberg, the creator and showrunner for BoJack Horseman, states:

> If you were to take a technology like this and say, 'We're going to give this to artists and make their lives easier and make their artistic power even greater', I would say, 'Oh, that's really interesting'. But I don't trust the companies to do that...When you look at the larger applications of these technologies, companies and studios never want to use it to empower artists to make cooler stuff for the same amount of money. They want to make things cheaper, cut the artists out, pay people less, and use these technologies in a way that doesn't make the work better. (Quoted in Kinder 2024)

The role of the consumer in this negotiation remains paramount, as journalist Molly Kinder (2024) notes:

> Whether AI will augment or automate—and whether and how much workers benefit from those gains—is not preordained. It depends on the choices of consumers, investors, employers, and technologists; the capabilities of the technology; the demand for workers' skills; and the existence—or lack—of guardrails to protect workers.

It is not just markets and profits, though—AI could well do a better job of being human. Thinking again about Ishiguro's *Klara and the Sun*, I am drawn to the idea of AI and its ability to mimic the empathetic. Of course Klara is not real, she is an imagined future AI creation, one imagined by human author Ishiguro, but she raises the question of how it would impact the world if emotional intelligence were something that could be coded. If AI is programmed to respond as a 'conscious and sensitive person' I have no doubt AI might prove a more empathetic respondent than me (or my family, ha!) at times. What if it becomes more 'efficient' to outsource things like care and sympathy to AI? What if AI surpasses its creators not just in terms of functionality but as an entity capable of exhibiting kindness? And what does this mean for writing that is concerned with the human condition? Of course, these concerns are not new—think of Mary Shelley's *Frankenstein* (1818) and Ridley Scott's *Blade Runner* (1982), creative works that point to the real concern: not AI, but the humans behind its creation.

References

Barthes, Roland. 1970. S/Z. London: Jonathan Cape.

Campbell, D. T. 1960. Blind Variation and Selective Retention in Creative Thought as in Other Knowledge Processes. *Psychological Review* 67: 380–400. https://doi.org/10.1037/h0040373.

Csikszentmihalyi, M. 1988. Motivation and Creativity: Toward a Synthesis of Structural and Energetic Approaches to Cognition. *New Ideas in Psychology* 6: 159–176. https://doi.org/10.1016/0732-118X(88)90001-3.

de Botton, A. 1998. *How Proust Can Change Your Life*. Pan Macmillan.

Dinning, Jessica. 2024. Articulated in CACW390 'Creative Writing Major Project). August 8, 2024, University of Wollongong, NSW, Australia.

Dollinger, S. J., K. K. Urban, and T. A. James. 2004. Creativity and Openness: Further Validation of Two Creative Product Measures. Creativity *Research Journal* 16: 35–47. https://doi.org/10.1207/s15326934crj1601_4.

Doshi, Anil R., and Oliver Hauser. 2023. Generative Artificial Intelligence Enhances Creativity but Reduces the Diversity of Novel Content, August 8. SSRN. https://doi.org/10.2139/ssrn.4535536.

Gero, Katy Ilonka, Tao Long, and Lydia B. Chilton. 2023. Social Dynamics of AI Support in Creative Writing. *CHI '23: Proceedings of the 2023 CHI Conference on Human Factors in Computing Systems* 245: 1–15. https://doi-org.ezproxy.uow.edu.au/10.1145/3544548.3580782.

Hetherington, Paul. 2022. Creative Rewriting and Recontextualisation: Fluid and Shape-Shifting Literary Works. *New Writing*. 19 (1): 91–102.

Hubert, Kent, Kim Aw, and Darya Zabelina. 2024. The Current State of Artificial Intelligence Generative Language Models Is More Creative Than Humans on Divergent Thinking Tasks. *Scientific Reports* 14, Article number: 3440.

Ishiguro, Kazuo. 2021. *Klara and the Sun*. London: Bloomsbury.

James, H. 1884. The Art of Fiction. *Longman's Magazine*, September. Reprinted in M. D. Zabel, ed: *The Portable Henry James*. 1951. New York: Viking, 391–418.

Jones, C., S. Svejenova, J. S. Pedersen, and B. Townley. 2016. Misfits, Mavericks, and Mainstreams: Drivers of Innovation in the Creative Industries.

Organization Studies 37: 751–768. https://doi.org/10.1177/0170840616647671.

Kinder, Molly. 2024. Hollywood Writers Went on Strike to Protect Their Livelihoods from Generative AI. Their Remarkable Victory Matters for All Workers. *Brookings*, April 12. https://www.brookings.edu/articles/hollywood-writers-went-on-strike-to-protect-their-livelihoods-from-generative-ai-their-remarkable-victory-matters-for-all-workers/#:~:text=A%20historic%20contract%20with%20new,major%20victory%20for%20the%20writers. Accessed August 12, 2024.

Kingsolver, Barbara. 2014. The Authorized Site. http://www.kingsolver.com/faq/about-writing.html. Accessed September 24, 2014.

Kirkpatrick, Keith. 2023. Can AI Demonstrate Creativity. *Communications of the ACM* 66 (2): 21–23. https://dl.acm.org/doi/fullHtml/10.1145/3575665. Accessed August 5, 2024.

Kris, E. 1952. *Psychoanalytic Explorations in Art*. New York: International University Press.

Leffer, Lauren. 2023. The AI Boom Could Use a Shocking Amount of Electricity. *Scientific American*, October 13. https://www.scientificamerican.com/article/the-ai-boom-could-use-a-shocking-amount-of-electricity/.

Lohr, Steve. 2024. A.I. Can Write Poetry, but It Struggles with Math. *New York Times*, July 23. https://www.nytimes.com/2024/07/23/technology/ai-chatbots-chatgpt-math.html?smid=nytcore-ios-share&referringSource=articleShare. Accessed July 31, 2024.

Margalit, Liraz. 2016. What Screen Time Can Really Do to Kids' Brains. Psychology Today, April 17. https://static1.squarespace.com/static/605d6ec761f05f07d68ec83a/t/64edac95c237f65764f1bc93/1693297813744/2_What+Screen+Time+Can+Really+Do+to+Kids%27+Brains+%7C+Psychology+Today.pdf. Accessed August 10, 2024.

Maslow, A. 1967. The Creative Attitude. In *Explorations in Creativity*, ed. R. L. Mooney and T. A. Rasik, 43–57. New York: Harper & Row.

Muppalla, Sudheer Kumar, Sravya Vuppalapati, Apeksha Reddy Pulliahgaru, and Himabindu Sreenivasulu. 2023. Effects of Excessive Screen Time on Child Development: An Updated Review and Strategies for Management. *Cureus* 15 (6, June): e40608. https://doi.org/10.7759/cureus.40608.

Oxford English Dictionary. 2024. https://www.oed.com/dictionary/learn_v?tab=meaning_and_use#39572078. Accessed on July 31, 2024.

Phelan, James. 1989. *Reading People, Reading Plots*. Chicago: University of Chicago Press.

Poulet, Georges. 1969. Phenomenon of Reading. *New Literary History* 1 (1): 53–68.

Rich, Simon. 2023. I'm a Screenwriter. These AI Jokes Give Me Nightmares. *Time*, August 4.

Roose, Kevin. 2024. The Data That Powers A.I. Is Disappearing Fast. *New York Times*, July 19. https://www.nytimes.com/2024/07/19/technology/ai-data-restrictions.html. Accessed on August 7, 2024.

Scott, Ridley (director). 1982. *Blade Runner*.

Secretaliasname. 2023. https://www.reddit.com/r/economy/comments/1ekrlu8/why_starbucks_is_losing_customers/. Accessed August 7, 2024.

Shelley, Mary. 1818. *Frankenstein*. London: Lackington, Hughes, Harding, Mavor & Jones.

Siemens, George. 2022. Not Everything We Call AI Is Actually 'Artificial Intelligence'. Here's What You Need to Know. *The Conversation*. https://theconversation.com/not-everything-we-call-ai-is-actually-artificial-intelligence-heres-what-you-need-to-know-196732. Accessed on July 31, 2024.

Taylor, Charles. 2024. https://www.forbes.com/sites/charlesrtaylor/2024/04/05/can-generative-ai-write-better-brand-music-than-humans/.

Twenge, Jean M., and W. Keith Campbell. 2018. Associations Between Screen Time and Lower Psychological Well-Being Among Children and Adolescents: Evidence from a Population-Based Study. *Preventive Medicine Reports* 12: 271–283. https://doi.org/10.1016/j.pmedr.2018.10.003.

Williams, Margery, and Gennady Spirin. 2017. *The Velveteen Rabbit*. Greenwood, Wisconsin: Suzeteo Enterprises.

Weber, M. 2023. Authors Are Resisting AI with Petitions and Lawsuits. *The Conversation*, July 26. https://theconversation.com/authors-are-resisting-ai-with-petitions-and-lawsuits-but-they-have-an-advantage-we-read-to-form-relationships-with-writers-208046. Accessed August 10, 2024.

Webster, E. Kipling, Corby K. Martin, and Amanda E. Staiano. 2019. Fundamental Motor Skills, Screen-Time, and Physical Activity in Preschoolers. *Journal of Sport and Health Science* 8 (2): 114–121. https://doi.org/10.1016/j.jshs.2018.11.006.

Winet, Evan Darwin. 2024. Email correspondence.

Darrin Hanna

Abstract **Darrin Hanna** says: computational tools are beginning to engage with the deeply personal, imaginative and affective dimensions of authorship. Machines now support authors by generating ideas, structuring plots, building characters and refining language use. However, AI's contributions to creative writing are derivative, powered by patterns not by lived experience. Probing the territory between authorship and assistance, we encounter ideas about originality and utility, about the speed of doing something and the depth of meaning in the thing or things we do. Here too we find questions about cognition, memory and emotion. While machines might simulate fluency, they do not feel or remember or truly understand. Positively however, AI, by lowering the barriers to doing creative writing, might encourage more people to write. Computational systems can become collaborators, as we adapt to them and adapt them to our needs—enhancing human creativity by unlocking time and offering structure and showing possibilities. The comparison most relevant to the relationship of AI to creative writing might be that of manmade furniture versus handcrafted furniture, highlighting the distinction between mass efficiency and bespoke artistry.

Keywords Simulation · Embodiment · Practice · Temporality · Tool

G. Harper (ed.), *AI and Creative Writing*,
https://doi.org/10.1007/978-3-031-99101-1_3

Dr. Darrin Hanna is a professor of Engineering at Oakland University, where he has specialized in artificial intelligence and embedded systems for more than 20 years. With a passion for innovative teaching, Dr. Hanna is dedicated to finding creative ways to engage students and support their learning journey. He has co-authored 18 books, many of which focus on the concept of learning by example, providing accessible and practical resources for students and professionals alike.

Beyond academics, Dr. Hanna has a keen interest in helping others bring their ideas to life. He has successfully licensed technologies, commercialized his own innovations, and assisted others in starting, growing, or scaling their businesses. As the founder of NextStep, a web-based software tool that helps individuals manage behavioral health challenges, he developed a practical solution aimed at improving care in an underrepresented healthcare sector. NextStep was later acquired by Connexin Software, a leading provider of pediatric healthcare software.

In his free time, Dr. Hanna has a range of personal interests that reflect his love for exploration and community. A licensed pilot and flight instructor, he enjoys flying small planes and takes pleasure in teaching his close friends and family members how to fly. His free time is often spent traveling, hosting gatherings with friends and family, and playing with his two Savannah cats.

Through his work at Oakland University and his various pursuits, he strives to inspire others to continue learning, exploring, and achieving their goals.

1. When someone says 'Artificial Intelligence' what things do you think about?

When someone says artificial intelligence, I immediately think of the incredible achievement of making a computer perform tasks that we typically associate with human intelligence. It's like watching a machine learn to think, reason, and make decisions, which still feels like a small miracle every time it happens.

Artificial intelligence is, at its roots, creations from humankind that allow machines to mimic human cognitive functions—everything from understanding language, recognizing patterns, making decisions, and even creating content. It's about taking the raw processing power of computers and shaping it into something that can interact with the world in a way that feels almost human.

What fascinates me most about AI is how it manages to bridge the gap between the purely logical, rule-based world of computers and the more intuitive, nuanced world of human thought. AI doesn't just follow rigid instructions; it learns from data, adapts to new situations, and can even surprise us with ideas we wouldn't have considered.

The development of AI is a testament to human ingenuity—our ability to create systems that can think and act in ways that are increasingly indistinguishable from human behavior. It's about understanding the essence of intelligence and finding ways to replicate it in a machine. This achievement isn't just about technology; it's about expanding our understanding of what it means to be intelligent and how that can be applied in new and innovative ways. It's not just about making machines more capable; it's about making them more like us, in a way that enhances our capabilities and expands our potential. The fact that we can create something that learns, adapts, and interacts with the world in a human-like way is a powerful reminder of how far we've come in our quest to understand and replicate intelligence, a journey that feels as magical as it is scientific.

2. Thinking of antonyms of 'intelligence', would it be possible, do you think, to have 'Artificial Unintelligence' or 'Artificial Stupidity' or 'Artificial Awkwardness' and, if so, what might they look like?

Yes, concepts like 'Artificial Unintelligence', 'Artificial Stupidity', or 'Artificial Awkwardness' could exist, intentionally designed to mimic suboptimal decision-making or socially awkward behavior. For example, Artificial Unintelligence might involve a system that deliberately makes poor choices or misunderstands instructions, useful in simulations or educational tools. Artificial Stupidity could simulate common errors or flawed logic for training. Artificial Awkwardness might recreate socially uncomfortable interactions, helping users practice navigating difficult social situations or even relating to a socially awkward or person with a social impairment. These systems could serve specific purposes, like training, humor, or illustrating the importance of intelligence and social awareness.

3. What kinds of things can AI help creative writers do? What kind of AI might help them best?

AI can be a powerful tool for creative writers, offering support at various stages of the writing process from idea generation to final edits. One of the primary ways AI can assist writers is through idea generation and brainstorming. AI can provide writing prompts, generate plot twists, or suggest unique character traits, sparking creativity when a writer feels stuck. Tools like GPT-based models are handy for generating story ideas, character backstories, or dialogue snippets based on themes or keywords.

AI can also help with character development. It can create detailed character profiles, backgrounds, and motivations, helping writers flesh out their characters. AI can simulate or check conversations between characters, helping to develop and ensure realistic and engaging dialogue. When it comes to plot structuring, AI can propose conflicts, challenges, and resolutions, offering alternative directions for a story to take. This allows writers to explore different narrative possibilities.

Writing and editing are other areas where AI proves invaluable. AI can expand on existing text, add details, or extend narratives, helping writers develop their stories more fully. It can also match a writer's style, generating content that maintains a consistent voice throughout the piece. AI can also help with world-building, especially in fantasy or science fiction genres. It can generate detailed settings, including world history, geography, and culture, creating immersive and believable fictional worlds. AI can also assist with grammar, punctuation, and spelling, allowing writers to focus on creativity rather than technical details. For those struggling with writer's block, AI can offer a way forward by suggesting what might come next in a stalled project or providing alternative phrasings. This helps writers overcome creative obstacles and maintain momentum.

AI would help creative writers save time, allowing them to complete their works more quickly—often far more quickly. This can lead to earlier releases of much-anticipated books, satisfying eager readers sooner. Imagine if AI had been available during the creation of the Harry Potter series. With AI's assistance, J.K. Rowling might have been able to release the books more quickly, perhaps even adding two more volumes to the beloved series. AI's role in streamlining the writing process doesn't just benefit the writers; it has the potential to expand the creative universe of stories and characters that fans love.

One of the most valuable advancements AI offers is its ability to help us complete tasks notably more efficiently, giving us back our most precious resource: time.

The best AI for creative writers includes natural language processing (NLP) models, character and plot generators, editing and grammar tools, and idea generators.

4. What things can AI not help creative writers do? (and this could be specifically associated with their writing or more generally in their lives)

While AI offers many valuable assets to assist creative writers, there are still several areas where it is limited, struggles, or currently falls short.

First, original inspiration and deep creativity are areas where AI struggles. While AI can generate ideas and mimic creative patterns, it lacks the true spark of human innovation. It cannot have epiphanies or create something entirely original, as it relies on existing data and patterns. Additionally, AI lacks the emotional depth and complexity that come from actual human experiences, making it difficult to capture the subtle nuances of human feelings in a way that resonates deeply with readers.

When it comes to personal voice and style, AI can't replicate the authentic voice that reflects a creative writer's individuality. Each writer's voice is shaped by their unique experiences and worldview—something AI cannot mimic. Personal and emotional challenges also lie beyond AI's capabilities. It can't provide the emotional support or resilience needed to cope with rejection, criticism, or self-doubt.

Life experiences and perspectives are crucial to authentic storytelling, and AI cannot replicate these. AI does not live a life, experience the world, or have memories, all of which are essential to creating rich, authentic narratives. AI cannot form or understand the complexities of human relationships, which are vital to developing compelling characters and stories.

In the realm of ethical and moral decision-making, AI is limited as well. It cannot engage with complex ethical dilemmas or make moral judgments, nor can it understand the societal impact or cultural significance of a piece of writing—areas where human insight is essential.

Authentic human connection is something AI cannot replicate. The bond between a writer and their readers, built on shared experiences and emotions, is deeply personal and beyond AI's reach. AI cannot completely replace the real, human interactions that occur in creative collaborations, where exchanging ideas and negotiating creative differences are essential.

5. If you knew a novel, or a poem or a screenplay was written using AI would it make any difference to how you responded to it as a reader or audience? Does the form of writing make any difference to your response—so, for example, if you knew a film you were watching had a script written using AI or, alternatively, if you were reading a novel written using AI? Does genre make any difference—for example, if you were reading a sonnet or an elegy, or if you were reading a science fiction short story, or if you were reading a video game script for an adventure game?

When considering whether knowing a novel, poem, or screenplay was written using AI would affect my response as a reader or audience member, it's important to recognize that we already consume a vast amount of content created by people we don't know and will never meet. We read sonnets, science fiction stories, and self-help books without knowing the authors personally. Similarly, we watch movies and TV series written by hidden figures whom we'll likely never encounter in real life. The connection we feel to the content is typically tied to the story, emotions, and ideas conveyed, rather than the identity of the creator.

This situation is somewhat analogous to how furniture is made today. Historically, furniture was meticulously handcrafted by skilled woodworkers, each piece bearing the unique touch of its maker. Today, the majority of furniture is produced by machines, enabling faster manufacturing and wider accessibility. Yet, for those who value the distinctiveness and craftsmanship of handmade pieces, such options remain available, at a higher cost and with longer waiting periods. Similarly, AI in creative writing could be seen as a tool to streamline the production of content, allowing for quicker access to new books, scripts, and poems.

One significant advantage of using AI in creative writing is the potential to speed up production timelines. We often have to wait a long time for the next season of a favorite series to be released or for an author's next book to hit the shelves. If AI could accelerate this process without sacrificing quality, it would be a major benefit to eager audiences.

Just as we accept machine-made furniture for its convenience and affordability while still appreciating the craftsmanship of handmade pieces, we might similarly embrace AI-generated content for its efficiency, particularly if it allows for quicker access to high-quality content, while still leaving room for those who seek the unique touch of human-crafted works.

6. Does any AI have imagination? If so, in way or ways? It not, why not? Do you believe it could ever have imagination?

Traditionally, imagination is the ability to create new ideas, images, or concepts that aren't directly based on what we've seen or experienced before. It's about making something original by combining knowledge and experiences in new ways. Human imagination is connected to our emotions, personal experiences, and consciousness, allowing us to create unique and meaningful things.

AI, as it exists today, doesn't have imagination in the same way humans do. AI models, like GPT-4, work by analyzing large amounts of data, finding patterns, and generating content based on those patterns. When AI creates something 'new', it's actually rearranging existing information in ways that might seem imaginative but are rooted in what it has already been trained on. AI doesn't have personal experiences, emotions, or a sense of self, so it can't truly imagine something entirely original like a human can.

That said, AI can still produce results that seem imaginative. AI can mix different ideas or styles that humans might not usually put together. AI can also introduce randomness into its output, creating content that isn't an exact copy of anything else. AI sometimes solves problems in unexpected ways, which can appear imaginative. For instance, in games, AI might develop new strategies that surprise even experienced players. These can lead to creative and surprising results that feel imaginative, even if they are based on existing data.

The idea of AI developing real imagination is still uncertain. For now, while AI can create content that seems imaginative, it doesn't have the true creative spark that comes from human experience and emotion.

7. The previous question touched on the notion of whether AI can itself be imaginative. The follow up, then, is whether it can (itself) form new ideas, have sensations, form memories? Can AI actually think? Can it feel?

AI doesn't invent ideas from scratch; it relies on patterns and knowledge it has been fed. While the outputs might appear novel, AI doesn't form new ideas in the way humans do. AI cannot have sensations. Sensations are linked to having a physical body with sensory organs that experience the world, such as seeing, hearing, or touching. AI processes data, but it doesn't 'see' or 'hear' in a conscious way. It can analyze visual or auditory data, but it has no subjective experience or awareness of this information.

AI can store and retrieve information, which might seem like forming memories, but this is different from human memory. Human memories are tied to personal experiences, emotions, and a sense of self. AI stores data in a structured way and retrieves it when needed, but it doesn't have personal experiences or a continuous identity. So, while AI can use past data, it doesn't form memories.

AI can process information, analyze data, and solve problems, but it doesn't 'think' as humans do. Human thinking involves consciousness, self-awareness, and the ability to reason abstractly. AI follows algorithms and models to perform tasks resembling thinking, like making decisions or predictions, but it does so without understanding or consciousness. AI's 'thinking' is mechanical, based on patterns, not conscious thought.

AI cannot feel. Emotions are complex and involve biochemical processes in the brain and body, as well as subjective experiences. AI can simulate emotions but it doesn't experience feelings. Any emotional response from AI is a programmed output, not a true feeling.

8. It might have been impossible for someone from the medieval period, where the quill was the primary writing tool and parchment the medium, to imagine a world in which word processors existed. Speculating as much as you like, what do you imagine the writing world will look like in 20 years, 50 years, and 200 years?

Speculating far into the future is much like trying to predict the weather in a specific city months or years in advance—uncertain and unreliable. While it's intriguing to imagine what the distant future might hold, it's more important to focus on the present reality: change is happening, and it's accelerating at an unprecedented rate, especially with AI.

In a world where AI and other technologies are reshaping many aspects of life, including writing, the key to thriving isn't predicting the future, but being prepared to adapt to it—whatever it may bring. This mindset will allow us to navigate the unknown and make the most of the opportunities that new technologies present, ensuring that we remain creative, relevant, and resilient in the face of change.

9. If you had all the time you needed, what written work would you like to write and why? It doesn't have to be a work of creative writing. Would you use AI to write it; and, if so, how would you use it?

If I had all the time I needed, I would write a book titled '10 Deadly Habits of the Most Successful Engineers: Saving Them From Themselves'. This book would draw from my collective experience in starting a business, merging technology companies, serving as chief architect of a tech company, and turning around a tech company on the verge of bankruptcy. It would explore the common pitfalls that highly successful engineers and programmers often encounter, particularly as they advance in their careers. The focus would be on how these 'deadly habits,' while contributing to early success, can lead to burnout, team dysfunction, or even career derailment if not managed properly.

The book would aim to provide insights into building and sustaining high-performing engineering and programming teams. It would delve into the art of cultivating a team culture where members feel valued, motivated, and eager to stay. This is crucial in an industry where retaining and engaging top talent is often as challenging as attracting it. The goal would be to offer practical advice on how to evolve these teams, fostering an environment where productivity is high, and people are genuinely satisfied with their work and work family.

I would consider using AI in the writing process to assist with research, idea generation, and helping me to articulate my ideas through quality writing with fewer iterations and more quickly than I typically could. AI could also aid in refining the book's structure and ensuring the content is engaging and accessible. However, the core message and insights would be deeply rooted in personal experience and human understanding, with AI serving as a valuable tool rather than the primary creator.

10. Who benefits most from using AI? Anyone more than anyone else? Any industry more than any other industry? Any place or places in the world? Do you think more people or fewer people might write creatively because of the existence and application of AI—if so, why; if not, why not?

AI benefits many industries and regions. Industries like technology, healthcare, finance, and manufacturing could benefit most from AI. In tech, AI can enhance productivity by automating tasks and improving software development. Healthcare can benefit from better diagnostics, personalized medicine, and efficient operations. In finance, AI could improve data analysis, risk management, and fraud detection. Manufacturing can see gains in production efficiency, predictive maintenance, and supply chain optimization. Developed countries with advanced technological infrastructure, such as the United States, Europe, and parts of Asia, benefit most, leveraging AI for innovation and economic growth.

Regarding creative writing, AI will certainly lead to more people writing by lowering barriers to entry, helping novice writers or those who are slow writers or write poorly develop ideas and refine their style. However, the ease of AI-generated content might also discourage some, as it could lead to content saturation and increased competition. This is akin to how the rise of self-publishing has democratized book publishing, making it accessible to anyone and resulting in a surge of new titles. While this has led to content saturation and information overload, it has also introduced new voices to the literary world. Despite the overwhelming volume of content, the industry has adapted through mechanisms like star ratings and reviews, which help readers navigate the vast selection. These systems allow quality work to rise to the top, enabling readers to discover valuable content amidst the abundance, and ensuring that the market remains viable and rewarding for talented authors.

Kristina Wright

Abstract **Kristina Wright** says: the meanings of 'artificial' and 'intelligence' point us toward the idea that AI simulates but does not replicate human cognitive and emotional capacities. Though it possesses speed and is able to recognize patterns, AI lacks consciousness, morality or subjectivity (including, therefore, feelings, taste and opinions). While it might have artificial intelligence it can also have artificial *un*intelligence—perpetuating systemic biases, as well as offering flawed decision-making and bad data in that 'data-trash in, output-trash out' way. It can, however, support a creative writer's brainstorming, research and editing. A useful tool, and a time saver, we should nevertheless not become over-reliant on AI. To do so would dilute originality and suppress the rich potential and complexity of the human imagination. In an increasingly digitized and commercialized writing world, more commercial genre and multimedia creative writing will likely benefit most, while emotionally resonant work in forms such as poetry not so much. Such emotional resonant, human-created works of creative writing will likely become more valued because of their rarity. Along with some redefining of value and practice in creative writing, AI also means a contemporary consideration of ethical issues associated with authenticity and with attribution and the potential for the undermining of forms of labor, which provide individuals and communities with livelihoods. Ultimately, human empathy, memory and mortality is irreplaceable in creative writing, even as AI transforms general writing tools and the landscape in which writing occurs.

G. Harper (ed.), *AI and Creative Writing*,
https://doi.org/10.1007/978-3-031-99101-1_4

Keywords Simulation · Authorship · Embodiment · Knowledge · Agency

Kristina Wright is a professor of English at Southern New Hampshire University, where she teaches creative writing, literature, and composition and rhetoric. She holds a PhD and an MA in English from Tufts University and a BA in English and creative writing from the University of North Carolina. Her research and teaching interests include the intersections of multimodal creative writing, composition, and digital media literacies. She is co-editor of *Multimodal and Digital Creative Writing Pedagogies* with Lexington Books/Rowan and Littlefield, and the author of several articles on the subject of teaching, including 'The Road Retaken: (Re)mix for Revision in Creative Writing' in *New Writing: The International Journal for the Practice and Theory of Creative Writing*, and 'Show Me What You Are Saying: Visual Literacy in the Composition Classroom' in *Visual Imagery, Metadata, and Multimodal Literacies Across the Curriculum*. Other areas of interest include creative non-fiction, poetry, and studies in American women's literature. Her poetry and creative non-fiction have appeared in *The Worcester Review*, *The Midwest Quarterly*, *Hippocampus Magazine*, *Brain, Child Magazine*, *Literary Mama*, *Sanskrit Literary Arts Journal*, among others. She is currently writing a creative non-fiction work from the perspective of her ancestor, Mary Parker Ayers, executed during the seventeenth century Salem Witch Trials, and a literary article about the nineteenth century U.S. author (and pseudonymously named) Fanny Fern.

1. When someone says 'Artificial Intelligence' what things do you think about?

I like to start with the meaning of words. 'Artificial' can mean something that simulates or imitates a natural phenomenon, like artificial sweeteners, or it can imply something that pretends to be real, such as emotions simulated by a robot. 'Intelligence' refers to the ability to make decisions based on knowledge to achieve an intended outcome. Combined, 'artificial intelligence' means computer systems trained with knowledge from large data sets, algorithms, and complex computations to *replicate or simulate* some of the cognitive tasks of human intelligence, such as decision-making. For me, this machine-form of intelligence is 'artificial' for two primary reasons—though both relate to its not-human-like behavior (in my mind). On the one hand, AI's ability to simulate human-brain cognitive tasks—like synthesizing vast amounts of information—is extraordinarily fast. What might take me weeks or months to process, takes AI mere seconds. If I possessed AI's level of fast processing of information, I'm sure I'd be considered superhuman. On the other hand, AI lacks many of the nuanced, subjective—psychological, intuitive, conscious, physical, or emotional—experiences of human decision-making. For example, an AI self-driving car avoids driving into oncoming traffic not out of a desire for self-preservation or fear of a crash, but because it has been programmed to do so. Whereas humans may avoid driving into oncoming traffic because they've learned the rules of the road, but also, perhaps, for subjective reasons, like the moral conscience to preserve human life or the emotional fear of a car crash. For this latter reason, computer intelligence is 'artificial' because it only imitates or *feigns* the subjective *reasons* humans use in their decision-making processes. Here I'm referring to *narrow AI*—as I understand it—technology that works by recognizing patterns in data and generating outputs based on those patterns to complete tasks. I am not referring to the still-theoretical concept of *general AI*, which could potentially have more complex meaning-making capabilities.

When I think of artificial intelligence in the context of generating creative writing, it seems like a highly advanced, time-efficient tool that might *assist* or *imitate* creative writers. It can automate repetitive tasks, generate text at lightning speed, and mimic writing styles, but it lacks the nuanced understanding of myriad, subjective, conscious (or unconscious) motivations and physically embodied senses that human writers bring to their creative work. Just as a camera with filters can create stunning images but it doesn't understand the story behind them, AI can assist in writing but doesn't really understand the story behind them or understand any of the motivations for narrating that piece of writing like a human might—hence, its 'artificialness'.

2. Thinking of antonyms of 'intelligence', would it be possible to have 'Artificial Unintelligence' or 'Artificial Stupidity', and, if so, what might they look like?

Yes, I think artificial unintelligence manifests as flawed decision-making due to bad data or programming. AI can analyze a vast amount of text, learn from it, and produce content that might seem intelligent on the surface. However, as I alluded to in my first answer, it doesn't have the conscious or moral understanding of its own content. It's like teaching a parrot to recite poetry; the parrot might say the words, but it doesn't understand the meaning behind them. Thus, like the parrot, AI can be unintelligent when it blindly repeats flawed data. For instance, AI, in its current state, can perpetuate biases and make harmful decisions if it operates on inaccurate or biased data. AI is only as intelligent as the data it parrots or learns from, and the risk of 'artificial unintelligence' arises when AI lacks the understanding to know when its own data may be flawed. To me, then, artificial *unintelligence* is data-trash in and output-trash out, so to speak.

If artificial intelligence is about teaching machines to think like humans, then these machines can also be programmed with the same kinds of flawed thinking based on bad data to which some humans are susceptible. For instance, AI may repeat biased language based on learning models that contain racist or sexist language without any qualms about the ethics of repeating this language or any empathy about the emotional impact on those targeted by this language. Artificial unintelligence happens if computers inadvertently perpetuate human systemic biases, not just in terms of flawed decision-making, but in reinforcing harmful societal biases in the language or ideas it replicates. Therefore, it's important to keep in mind that narrow AI is a generative tool, and in its current iteration—as far as I understand— is only as intelligent as the data sets it learns from. Therefore, a human ought to be careful not to rely too heavily on AI's recommendations without ever questioning them. Know your sources. In short, artificial *unintelligence* means parroting flawed thinking or bad data.

3. What kinds of things can AI help creative writers do? What kinds of AI might help them best?

AI can be a good *tool* for writers, especially in the early stages of writing for generating ideas or overcoming writer's block. AI can act like a writing assistant who can help writers jumpstart ideas for their work. For instance, if you're stuck on a plot point, AI can suggest different directions based on existing storytelling patterns or even from questions the author asks it. AI can brainstorm with a writer, much like a creative writing partner or writing coach might. Let's say you're stuck trying to figure out how a character should respond in a tense situation. Your AI assistant might suggest a few possible reactions based on the character's established traits—helping you see options you hadn't thought of. The writer is still in control of the narrative, but AI can offer suggestions based on overlooked patterns (like another human reader of one's work might). The writer is always free to ignore unhelpful suggestions, too.

AI is also useful for handling research quickly. For example, if you're writing a novel set in a specific historical period, AI can help by researching relevant information or fact-check for anachronistic language or suggest authentic details for that period. It's like having a research assistant, with instant access to huge libraries from all over the world, who's lightning quick and efficient at compiling data for the writer to use in their work. AI can further help with proofreading tasks, such as editing for grammar, checking for grammatical consistency, or summarizing lengthy texts.

AI can also be used as a template tool, say, for outlining chapters for a novel or for storyboarding a screenplay. But I think today's AI goes well beyond basic outlining or storyboarding capabilities to act as a digital writing assistant. Arguably, an AI writing assistant may support beginning writers learning their craft or more advanced authors who cannot afford a professional writing coach, or don't have a writers' group to read their work and suggest feedback. In other words, today's AI writing assistants can offer authors some of the collaborate drafting and writing advice that was once the sole domain of human writing coaches, research assistants, editors, writers' groups, and creative writing teachers.

4. What things can AI not help creative writers do? (and this could be specifically associated with their writing or more generally in their lives).

While AI can assist in the writing and researching process, it doesn't replace the need for human judgment, creativity, originality, conscious awareness, or emotional insight. It's a tool that can help writers produce work more efficiently, but it's not a substitute for the writing process entirely. Writers might see AI as a collaborator, one that can handle research, brainstorming, and even basic drafting. But it can't replace the core creative work of the author. I feel, very strongly, in fact, that writers should not completely give over their creative powers to a machine. To me, it's the difference between, say, getting some feedback from a writing coach versus asking the writing coach to write your manuscript entirely. Moreover, I'd caution writers to avoid overlying on AI, even for some of those drafting basics mentioned. The speedy efficiency of AI is tempting to use; yet the drafting and invention phase of writing are fertile phases. In other words, handle AI's power with care lest your own power wanes. Relying too much on AI to generate content could potentially stifle creativity by leading writers to conform to imitative patterns suggested by AI, reducing originality. Creative writers ought to be careful about letting machines produce their writing lest we humans begin to sound like machines—and not the other way around!

If using AI as a digital writing assistant, writers should be mindful they may not always get, what I consider to be, the fruitful, subjective feedback of another human reader. Sure, AI can proofread, but what about how the draft *resonates* with another human—the audience, for whom, presumably, the writer is writing? I believe something essential to the human experience may be lost in translation if one's only feedback during drafting is exclusively from a computer-generated writing assistant. But perhaps that's my own quirky luddite-ism or nostalgia about the uniqueness of human empathy.

Additionally, if creative writers use AI as writing assistant tools, there are ethical issues that arise. Traditionally, authors write an acknowledgements section in a book to credit to people—editors, research assistants, writers groups, etc.—who helped them with the content. But what about the parts of one's book that were AI-generated? From what I understand, this is a hotly debated subject. AI-generated content may infringe on copyright and unethically—even illegally—poach existing human intellectual property to generate content. Thus, use of AI-generated writing brings up ethical, legal, originality, citation, and economic considerations about the proprietary nature of creative work.

Along these lines, there may be a quality control issue in AI-generated advice. An AI writing assistant may not be generating top quality advice based on top quality literary data. Remember my comment about artificial unintelligence? Trash in, trash out? Additionally, AI as a proofreader may insert flawed editing. Consider how spell-check autocorrects words in unwanted ways. The writer must be careful AI is not generating unwanted grammar advice. Let's say, a writer deliberately writes a character as someone who uses 'incorrect' grammar as part of how that character speaks, then the writer should be wary of letting AI uniformly autocorrect all the grammar in the manuscript as this would ruin that character's speech patterns.

5. If you knew a novel, poem or screenplay was written using AI would it make any difference to how you responded to it as a reader or audience? Does the form of writing make any difference to your response—So, for example, if you knew a film you were watching had a script written using AI? Does genre make any difference—for example, if you were reading a sonnet or an elegy, a science fiction short story, or a video game script for a game?

Yes, knowing that a piece of writing is AI-generated influences how I respond to it, particularly as a writing professor. In a college setting, it's challenging to provide meaningful feedback on creative content that I suspect has been generated by AI but presented as original student work. While this raises concerns about academic integrity, including potential plagiarism, academic-setting privacy rules and the limitations of AI-detection tools require me to approach these situations with care. To address these complexities, I establish clear guidelines on the appropriate use of AI in our creative writing classroom, trusting students to follow these standards. So, in the context of being a teacher-reader of student writing, then who—or what—wrote the work matters greatly.

But outside the context of being a teacher-reader, when I am a reader-audience for my personal consumption of creative works, the genre plays more of a role in how much it matters. For example, I wouldn't want to hear an AI-written eulogy at a funeral; I'd want to hear the heartfelt words of the bereaved. Similarly, when reading a poem, I want to hear the unique voice and inventive language of the author. Take Edgar Allan Poe's *The Raven*, for instance. I imagine Poe by candlelight, quill in hand, channeling a tale of grief through powerful language. An AI-generated poem in Poe's style might be an interesting replica, but it would lack the authenticity of his inventiveness, ringing hollow for me. It may *evoke* emotions in me, as the reader, but I'd feel a bit cheated to discover a machine wrote it because it was not written from a place of human ingenuity and empathy. Kind of like the parrot analogy—a parrot might recite Poe's poem, but it doesn't know the meaning of the words it is repeating. As a reader, I want a communal exchange with the author of a creative work. When I read a Poe poem, I know the author is long-deceased, yet he is immortalized in the words of his poem. I love the idea of authorship being a form of immortality for humans precisely because we are mortal. A machine does not die (unless you unplug it, I suppose) but it does not die like a mortal human. I am getting philosophical here, but I think I cannot connect as deeply with a machine-generated poem as I can with a human-created one because I inherently understand the precious nature of the author's mortal life being preserved, immortalized, in the words.

However, in multimedia storytelling, such as movies with AI-generated effects or video games, I'm more willing to accept AI-authored content as part of the technology used—similar to how lighting or sound are technologies. Poe's quill pen was his technology, but it was merely the medium through which he communicated his thoughts, not the thoughts themselves. An AI-generated 3D reenactment of Poe's poem might be a creative way to present his work, but the original creative content belongs to Poe, not the technology. Overall, I believe that creative writing, borne from human imagination, or, at least, empathetic consciousness (i.e. not merely parroting), is more valuable than an AI work. In traditional literary genres like memoirs, poems, novels, and eulogies, I value, especially, the human creator over AI. But in screen-based, multimedia genres, I'm more accepting of AI technology.

6. Does any AI have imagination? If so, in what ways? It not, why not? Do you believe it could ever have imagination?

It depends on one's definition of 'imagination'. If we consider imagination to be the ability to generate creative content on topics one hasn't experienced, then yes, AI could be seen as imaginative. For instance, the poet Emily Dickinson imagined and wrote about her own death, while she was alive. AI, too, can generate content on themes it hasn't experienced, like writing poem in the voice of death personified.

However, AI doesn't possess imaginative inventiveness in the way humans do. I believe human imagination is connected not only to consciousness and lived experiences but also to abstract thought. AI, in contrast, relies on pattern recognition, producing outputs by rearranging existing elements in novel ways. While this can mimic creativity,

AI doesn't create new ideas from scratch; it reconfigures and generates new patterns based on pre-existing ones (I think). Therefore, while AI can simulate creativity, I don't think it stems from the abstract richness of the human imagination. AI also lacks the self-awareness to know it's *imagining* something it hasn't experienced. For example, virtual assistants like Siri, Apple's human-sounding AI that works with voice recognition, might give witty responses, but it doesn't imagine the scenarios it describes. If you ask Siri a silly question, like, 'Do you know what it is to love?' Siri says something like, 'Well, I rather love what I am doing right now', so it's mimicking an imaginative human-like response based on programming and data patterns, but it is not imagining what it is enjoy one's work. At least, I don't think so.

That said, the line blurs when we consider AI-generated creative artifacts. For instance, a woman I knew sold abstract paintings her cat created by swishing its paint-covered tail across a canvas. The cat wasn't likely consciously imagining the artwork it produced, yet the paintings were considered art. Similarly, we might question whether the origin of a creative work—whether human or AI—matters if the creation itself resonates. In literary studies, we often separate the author's intent from the work itself, focusing on our interpretations. Perhaps the same could apply to AI-generated content, where the creation's impact transcends its non-human origin. Ultimately, as readers, the writing is most alive in *our imaginations*, which may be different from what the author— human or machine—imagined (or not) when writing it.

7. The previous question touched on the notion of whether AI can itself be imaginative. The follow up, then, is whether AI can (itself) form new ideas, have sensations, form memories? Can AI think? Can it feel?

I think AI can form new ideas since it can draw conclusions and predict patterns that it didn't previously know. Machine learning systems enable AI to learn from data, improving its performance over time and discovering more efficient ways to do its tasks. This ability can be seen as forming new ideas or generating new outputs. AI can also 'remember' tasks it has previously learned, much like I can play a piano piece from memory without looking at the music. We both do this from memorizing repetition of patterns, right? (I'm sure as a non-computer scientist, I am grossly simplifying AI's memory processes based on my own technical ignorance).

However, I'm not convinced AI can experience emotions or physical sensations evoked by music. It can simulate or replicate the effects of emotions, but I don't believe it would feel the emotions of playing music or the physical sensations evoked by hearing music, such as being moved to tears or inclined to dance, like a human might. Unlike humans, AI lacks consciousness and subjective experience. It cannot truly empathize with the emotions it mimics. So, no, it does not feel—emotionally or physically—I don't think.

8. It might have been impossible for someone from the medieval period, where the quill was the primary writing tool, to imagine a world in which word processors existed. Speculating as much as you like, what do you imagine the writing world will look like in 20 years, 50 years, and 200 years?

In the future, the writing 'tools' will be all computer-generated—whether through keyboard and screen, voice recognition, or computer chips implanted in human brains. I think in 100 years, no one will even know how to use a pen and paper. These tools won't exist anymore just as very few people today know how to use quill and ink. Writing by hand will become completely obsolete, as today's generation of school children are no longer taught how to write in cursive, at least in many parts of the United States, where access to digital technologies is ubiquitous. In parts of the world, where digital technologies and access to new tools for written communication are not readily available, economic inequalities in literacy access and knowledge will continue to deepen. Much like how generational divides are deepening today between digitally savvy youths and elders who were not educated in today's technology.

Businesses will prefer to use AI for repetitive, formulaic, or mundane writing tasks because AI does these tasks faster and never needs breaks, unlike human writer-employees. AI use will exploit the commercial side of creative writing, producing novels, stories, and screenplays because the machines won't get tired or expect royalties on their work. However, companies that provide AI software will profit from providing the technologies for these services. The drive for profit, as usual, will dominate the market, leading to significant consequences for human creative writers. I predict, too, data wars over proprietary intellectual property and the desire to preserve copyrights over human-created works will increase. It may spawn new copyright laws about fair use access to human literary models for AI data.

This shift will affect teaching academia and creative writing. If AI can quickly generate well-researched and properly cited academic papers, students may question the value of learning how to write such papers. Similarly, if AI can produce screenplays, short stories, and poems, students might wonder about the relevance of studying the craft of writing. This could undermine the importance of writing studies, leading to a devaluation of literacy education overall. It may lead to a derivative and expedient view of writing as product-based output and not as creative or careful expression of meaning or thoughts. However, educators may adapt by emphasizing process-based writing and critical thinking over the final product, which some are already doing. But the massive proliferation of AI-generated content likely represents a future erosion of human literacy and an increase in potential forms of fake news, knowledge control, and creative censorship. I suppose my vision for the future is rather Orwellian. But we see human literacy and open-minded exchange of ideas already eroded by reliance on digital technologies which promote censorship, anti-intellectualism, confirmation bias in news feeds, and other anti-freedom of expression politics.

On a positive note, human-generated content could become more valuable due to its rarity. Just as artisan-made furniture is valued over machine-made or mass-produced factory furniture, human-authored works might gain higher status compared to AI-generated content. The difference between the two could create a hierarchical value system, where human-generated works are seen as more desirable. If AI-generated works are the equivalent of factory-made furniture, human-authored works could be considered the artisan variety, potentially increasing their value. However, cheaper AI-generated content might appeal more than pricier human-authored content, like choosing less expensive furniture over artisan options for economic reasons. I may prefer a human-authored work, but perhaps I cannot afford it. This economic disparity might influence the quality and consumption of creative works, leading to a dystopian scenario where economics may shape the quality and accessibility of creative content in practical, somewhat disturbing ways. Using a more hopeful outlook, I imagine new genres might emerge that blend human creativity with AI-generated content in innovative ways, offering exciting opportunities for both writers and readers—at least, I hope so.

9. If you had all the time you needed, what written work would you like to write and why? It doesn't have to be a work of creative writing. Would you use AI to write it; and, if so, how would you use it?

I write some poetry, but mostly memoir. Due to time constraints, I tend to write essay-length memoirs. If time were no issue, I'd write a book-length family history as I have some incredible family lore. This would require a lot of research. For example, I'd like to write about how my great grandfather, a brilliant, but eccentric man from France, ended up in a mental health institution in Winnipeg, Manitoba in the 1920s. The institution is no longer standing and no one who knew him is still alive. I want to write an accurate portrayal of what life may have been like for him in that institution. AI could assist me in compiling research on that place or how people who were assumed to have mental illness were typically treated based on 1920s' psychiatry practices. I might use AI for the purposes of proofreading or fact-checking. At this point, however, I view AI primarily as research or editing tools, much like I view digital archives as research tools or grammar and spell-check as editing tools for proofreading my work. I would not write an entire creative work using only an AI proofreader; I'd ask a human reader to give me some feedback, too. Nor would I use AI to generate my creative content. I enjoy the pain and pleasure of writing from my own imagination, experiences, emotions, and thoughts. I enjoy the inventive act of producing something written that is uniquely my own.

10. Who benefits most from using AI? Anyone more than anyone else? Any industry more than any other industry? Any place or places in the world? Do you think more people or fewer people might write creatively because of the existence and application of AI—if so, why; if not, why not?

While every conceivable industry will be touched in some way by the impact of AI technology, the benefits of AI seem most obvious in the technology, healthcare, scientific research, transportation, ecommerce, and finance industries. Also, in industries that rely on repetitive labor practices, such as manufacturing. Just as the xerox machine replaced the need for professional scriveners to manually copy out written legal documents, so, too, will AI benefit industries that rely on efficiency and productivity in completing repetitive manual labor or rote mental tasks. If AI and automation continues to replace repetitive human labors (whether physical or mental), it will have wide-ranging consequences for those people whose livelihood depends on such labors.

AI will have future, seismic shifts, I think, in the field of education, in all disciplines, including literacy education. As for creative writing, the future impact of AI and automation given its magnitude is hard to fathom. AI is a powerful tool that can both streamline creative work but may also render certain creative skills obsolete. The lid on this technological Pandora's box is already lifted, so there's no shutting it again. We humans will need to proceed wisely as we unleash this potent, powerful technology into the world. From a dystopian standpoint, we ought to be careful not to let AI become Frankenstein's monster lest we regret inventing it in the first place. From a less gloomy perspective, AI will, perhaps, make our human lives easier in new and welcome ways. Or perhaps both. No doubt, the changes AI brings are irreversible, impacting our creative writing in ways we are only beginning to consider. I hope, in the process, we preserve, above all else, the best of our humanity.

References/Acknowledgements I wish to acknowledge that some of my understanding of how AI works (especially the distinction between Narrow AI, in its current iteration, and the theoretical idea of General AI) was explored during an informational interview with my colleagues: David Humphries, Director, AI Integration, and Dr. Shawn Powers, Senior Director AI Policy, Southern New Hampshire University. Though, all potential errors in my explanations are *entirely* my own.

Brooke Biaz

Abstract **Brooke Biaz** says: rather than reducing AI to a set of technological functions it can best be considered through the lens of emotion, memory, creative practice and cultural critique. AI offers conceptual provocation and ethical challenges. One conceptual provocation might well be the inaccuracy of the term 'artificial intelligence' itself, given that AI lacks sensation, intention and the capacity for embodied experience. Such things we have long associated with intelligence. More broadly, we do not quite have the range of philosophic, psychological and languages to fully explore and consider how AI relates to our understanding of human intelligence and creativity. AI's version of creativity is a simulation, and it cannot replicate the layered, relational and visceral processes that are core to creative writing. It can, however, assist with research, with writing structure and with modeling language, acting as a tool and as a mirror—that is, to enhance reflection of what we do and who we are. AI is incapable of replacing the socially and emotionally entangled act of creative writing, but today's bifurcated creative cultures influence creative writers and the readers and audiences for their works—some AI-enabled, and some intentionally human-driven. It is hoped, in this, we will not lose the personal satisfaction that many find in the human-centered creative process—whether as participants in creating or as audiences for creatively produced works. Complexity, presence and human action are central to the integrity of creative writing.

G. Harper (ed.), *AI and Creative Writing*,
https://doi.org/10.1007/978-3-031-99101-1_5

Keywords Machines · Artificiality · Intelligence · Integrity · Meaningfulness

Brooke Biaz is a fiction writer who spends a lot of time on the Communion Islands and lived there prior to emigrating to the USA in 2011. Brooke's recent works include *Robots and Other Stories* (Parlor, 2025) and *Releasing the Animals* (Parlor, 2023). Previous works include *The Japanese Cook* (Parlor, 2018), *The Invention of Dying* (Parlor, 2015), *Camera Phone* (Parlor, 2009) *Moon Dance* (Parlor, 2008) and *Small Maps of the World* (Parlor, 2006). Brooke, who sometimes writes as Graeme Harper, has also contributed to a number of exploratory works about creative writing and about higher education, and has been awarded such honors as the Norton Island Residency, along with writing, travel and research awards from the British Academy, UK Arts and Humanities Research Council, Australia Council, University of Texas Medical Branch, and Australian National Book Council, among others.

1. When someone says 'Artificial Intelligence' what things do you think about?

I first think about machines. It's the 'artificial' that makes me think that way. A little while later I think about depictions of machines in novels and in films. Of course, *The Terminator* (Cameron, 1984) immediately comes to mind. After that *I, Robot* (Proyas, 2004), a film I never seemed to be able to quite like, but have returned to two or three times, nevertheless. The question of trust keeps coming up in the film—not just between people and AI, but between who seek to use or profit from AI. AI in that way both supports and undermines humankind. I think of other films too. I think of a few lines from the poet Andrew Motion's poem 'Randomly Moving Particles' in his collection of the same name: 'My father when his body machinery is working, just / but his mind / he abandoned' (14) The poet is remembering his father on his deathbed. The juxtaposition of body and machine catches—much as the use of the word 'juxtaposition' after the use of the word 'deathbed'!

Artificiality seems to be difficult to care about. Once, when I was maybe 8 or 9 years of age, I found some artificial flowers in the cement gutter of a nearby street. Back then I spent a lot of time wandering the streets near my home, barefoot and in shorts, tanned in the sun. The streets were mostly paved, though some were still dirt. These two flowers were found on one of the paved streets, and they were a couple of dusty long-stemmed plastic flowers, with gray-green leaves. I recall one had a yellow bloom, perhaps imitating a dahlia, and the other had a few purple florets, perhaps aiming to be crocus. It is the feel of the flowers I recall most: the slippery, cold, plastic feel. The gray-greenery had nodules on, from where it was pulled from plastic molds, I guess. It was possibly to rub off the dust with your thumb. There of course was no aroma.

I'm noticing I have not addressed the word 'intelligence'. I think that's because I don't find intelligence to be artificial. Intelligence is natural and it is alive and it is touchable—like skin, figuratively speaking.

I guess I am saying that when someone says 'artificial intelligence' I don't see or hear the intelligence. In this way, I fundamentally disagree with the term. It is a label created at a point in time (when American scientists, mid-twentieth century, were seeking a label for something they were exploring) and its meaning, to me, is at best parodic an at worst simply false. I think to do 'AI' justice we need a better term for it. It might be, if we think about it further, that it is not intelligence. It might also be, if we think about how we might use it, that it is not entirely artificial, either.

2. Thinking of antonyms of 'intelligence', would it be possible, do you think, to have 'Artificial Unintelligence' or 'Artificial Stupidity' or 'Artificial Awkwardness' and, if so, what might they look like?

I might have already answered this....but the question nicely builds on my previous thoughts and I end up contemplating it, for sure, as my friend Alice walks into the kitchen. And, so, I say:

'Hey, Alice, a question . . . ?'

'Yes,' she says, and she says this as she is reaching out to pick out from the wire rack in which it hovers the last French Vanilla coffee pod in the house and as she, then, goes right ahead and pushes that pod into my single serve coffee maker.

I pause, taken aback a little, I admit, because, though I don't mention it often, I prefer French Vanilla over Columbian Dark Roast or, even more so, over French Medium Roast, and though occasionally considering the temporal appropriateness of it, also very much over the ill-defined 'Breakfast Coffee' which appears to be nobody's first choice, given most of the rack remains full of pods of it. Eventually, I say, as vanilla begins to emanate, out and around the kitchen:

'Oh, well,' I say, 'oh well, well.'

I don't cope well with conflict, but this situation is clearly outrageous.

'Awkwardness,' I say, and I suspect immediately I am revealing too much of how I am feeling.

'Yes,' she says, and the coffee maker is seething now, steaming now.

'Stupidity,' I say, loudly, for sure. There is only the two of us in the kitchen and though I give all my friends a key to my apartment, few of them use theirs. But Alice does. Alice does regularly, and now look what she's done.

'Unintelligence,' I say.

'Oh yes,' she says, now pouring her coffee. God, that smells good.

'AI,' I say, 'is it possible . . . for it to be . . .'

'Awkward?' she replies.

'Yes,' I say.

'Stupid and unintelligent?' She slumps down with her coffee into my second favorite armchair, by the bookcase, near the standard lamp shaped like a flamingo, across from me. 'Well...' she continues.

'Well?' I ask.

'Well, I don't know,' she says, 'it's a computer, right?'

And then it strikes me that if someone can misunderstand etiquette between friends maybe they can misunderstand a lot of other things. Maybe, also, then, if AI can only understand what we humans give it to understand, and even if, say, it comes to understand things on its own, there is no guarantee it will be supremely intelligent, and certainly no chance it will have an infallible understanding. In fact, we might consider whether volume of power to identify and analyze and interpret ever is also a firm guarantee of an ability to behave intelligently. In which case, maybe misconstrue what we expect from AI, and what we should expect. We also potentially misread what our relationship with it should be, and can be—not to solely use it as a tool, as such, but rather that we should be seeing it more as a co-presence, more than décor, but less than making a roommate, more than the sum of what we offer it, but forever less than human. Just as likely to be awkward, and stupid and unintelligent as any of us might be, but never forgivably so—and in that, potentially, more helpful to us as an occasional guide than as a companion.

3. What kinds of things can AI help creative writers do? What kind of AI might help them best?

AI can help creative writers think about what creative writing actually is. And I mean the existence of AI should, at very least, asks us to confirm (for ourselves and maybe for others) what we think creative writing entails as a human practice. It takes us to core values, core principles even, perhaps. If creative writing is simply the end of results of some kind of activity, and we don't care too much what that activity is, or even whether humans do it, mostly only that it ends up producing a poem or a story, a novel or a screenplay, then whether we use AI or a stick scrawling in mud is not as significant as what we (or someone else) thinks of the thing we complete. But if activity of creative writing is itself important to us—the mental and physical act of it, the particular visceral pursuit of it, the tangible, palpable condition of doing it, then what AI can help us do is defined by that fact.

Posing this, I say that AI can help us *be* creative writers, but it cannot help us *become* creative writers. That is, if we already have a relationship with creative writing then AI can provide enhancement of our understanding of why that relationship exists and what it entails, as well as, potentially, being a tool applied in our ongoing engagement with that relationship. However, if we think that the technical aspects of prompting AI Large Language Models to create simulations of written human language patterns will solely help us become creative writers, we're overstating the case. Not even if the end result is all that matters will that event occur, because creative writing is built by layered interaction within human beings and between human beings. However, the good news is, that it is in this layering AI can offer some help.

The best way AI can assist us (that is, creative writers) is to assist us to add to the layering of thought, imagination, observation, inscription that we undertake when doing creative writing. In that, it is very like any writing tool, but because generative AI also offers modeling of language patterns, and this kind of AI is capable of accessing a vast range of information, it can add to our layering of action and imaginative conjecture and thinking. Treat it like it is doing creative writing for us, however, and this contribution is undermined and our creative writing is diminished not supported.

4. What things can AI not help creative writers do? (and this could be specifically associated with their writing or more generally in their lives)

It cannot meet friends at the pub for lunch. It cannot drink coffee on a rainy day in London, looking out the window of the coffee shop at red double decker buses with steamy drizzled windows and people passing with harassed umbrellas or vinyl jackets pulled up and clasped over their heads, and the homeless under cardboard by the park fence, opposite, and the flashing orange light of black cabs depositing harried professionals and public school kids in uniforms and chunky shoes and hair dripping. It cannot make love to anyone or hold someone's hand for even a moment. It cannot decide to go out to smell the night air, just because it wants to. It cannot touch anything. It cannot lift a child over an iron gate to let them into a park and it does not truly know why it would want to. Oh, but boy can it help give the impression of creative writing happening, and in that simulacra, it can challenge and upset, disrupt and disturb, simulate and stimulate and set in inscribed relief what human written communication might appear to be. While it cannot help creative writers be themselves it can help them be what we think them to be, and in that it cannot help but be a version of what we might think creative writers to be, it cannot help but reveal our traditions, our beliefs, our thoughts, our prejudices and our hopes.

5. If you knew a novel, or a poem or a screenplay was written using AI would it make any difference to how you responded to it as a reader or audience? Does the form of writing make any difference to your response—so, for example, if you knew a film you were watching had a script written using AI or, alternatively, if you were reading a novel written using AI? Does genre make any difference—for example, if you were reading a sonnet or an elegy, or if you were reading a science fiction short story, or if you were reading a video game script for an adventure game?

If I knew a short story was written using crayons on torn sheets of Butcher Paper, I'd ponder the crayon strokes, their colors, and the size of the sheet. I'd look at the (likely) unevenness of the handwriting and consider the situations when one word was crossed out and another added, and why that might have been the case. I would read the whole thing and think about the story, with the compositional evidence in front of me. The same goes for something composed using AI—as far as having evidence in front of me goes, that is.

The nature of the evidence in the AI case, given there likely would be no record of the prompts given or of previous drafts composed via the Generative AI, would be less interesting (compositionally, speaking) to that in the crayon writing case. Less interesting even than the evidence of a poem composed (without AI) on a computer, for example, too, because (for me) I get pleasure out of imagining the creative writer working on a piece of writing. I get less pleasure, if any, out of reading a novel or a poem or a script where the compositional practices behind it have not involved as much direct, contemporaneous human activity as I am applying in reading or watching something. Even if the final work—whether novel, poem, short story, film or otherwise—is enjoyable, I find it less interesting and less pleasurable if it is not the result of direct, combinatory, unifying, concomitant engagement of a human or humans. And I just don't see AI composition working that way on its own, even though it draws on data (most of which is made by humans) and it imitates human written language use (analyzing what we have put out in the digital world for it to find) and it responses to our prompts, which we might refine to get the emerging work closer and closer to what we want, the nuances are not there, the compositional integrity is not there.

'Integrity' is a provocative choice of words, of course—given it suggests that the use of AI to write a film or novel or poem might lack honesty and virtue. I don't mean it that way. Rather, I am using 'integrity' to refer to the state of being whole, being complete. A creative composition in which my spelling has been checked by a machine (and my grammar sometimes flagged for me to consider) seems to me to continue to rely on my imaginative and writerly engagement with it to move from my thought or observation or feeling to a final work. A composition in which I pose a writing job to an AI Chatbot, and then react to its efforts, drawn from its knowledge of human language use; and I prompt it again, and maybe again and again and again, until its composition more matches my vision of what the piece of writing might ultimately be. That latter condition feels incomplete to me because components of the decision are reduced (I have less input at the micro level of the writing) and the physicality of the writing more quickly defines (in terms of on-screen inscription, of course) an object, rather than the trace of that object existing in my mind, and remaining there even after the composition is complete. This makes me less interested in works of creative writing produced largely by AI as well—no matter what genre they are in.

6. Does any AI have imagination? If so, in way or ways? It not, why not? Do you believe it could ever have imagination?

'Does a house brick know how it feels to make a house your home?' was once my response to these kinds of questions. I mean, back when LLMs started to gain more attention at the end of 2022, and it seemed the most pressing response was to mention the inanimate nature of AI 'intelligence'. It was a protective response on my behalf, of course. The idea of a machine taking over the imaginative work of a human being bothered me deeply. Shortly after that, I pretended to ask an AI chatbot if it had an imagination and I pretended it had responded in the affirmative. I then said: 'No, you don't.' (indignantly, of course) While my fictional Chatbot feigned being insulted, it also reminded me (fictionally, and without saying very much) that AI is more than clay and sand and water. Simply, such AI is no brick. If anything, it might be considered bricks in the hands of bricklayers, and it tries to simulate how those bricklayers (or a particular bricklayer) might think and act. It cannot feel, but those who prompt it can use words about feelings and instructions to feel to get it to draw linguistic codes (words, phrases, sentences that are associated with feeling) from the digital world and thus, in that way, it can emulate our feelings. This might or might not evoke your indignation! Incidentally, AI can also emulate indignation.

Given that the imagination involves feeling, understanding and memory AI can, un-brick-like as it is, give the impression it has a form of imagination by copying and adapting to task at hand what it finds out in the digital world. It can't have actual sensations, though it can draw on online versions of what we have said (and published) about sensations, over time. It can't actually feel, of course, and though its neural processing can be inspired by operations of the human brain, it has no actual emotions. But it can emulate, build from pictures placed in or drawn into the digital world, and mapped onto responses from humans it can find there too.

Artificial General Intelligence (AGI), were such thing to one day exist, might have a version of what we might call an imagination, but it won't drink coffee or eat chocolate or ever truly experience what 'puppy breath' is.

7. The previous question touched on the notion of whether AI can itself be imaginative. The follow up, then, is whether it can (itself) form new ideas, have sensations, form memories? Can AI actually think? Can it feel?

It can, in some way, 'think'. It cannot feel.

The way in which AI can think is that involving accessing and analyzing information and making decisions based on that information. It can draw on things out there in the world, and on its own cloud of information, as it were, and in this way, it draws on a kind of memory (and not narrowly in the computer science sense). But it has no ethics, unless we tell it to emulate ethics, and it has no sensory relationship with anything, unless we tell it to emulate one (and even then it only creates simulacra, of course). It can never experience or touch what the impact of its words might be on a reader or audience or perceive how it might create sensations for others, based on those it has personally experienced.

8. It might have been impossible for someone from the medieval period, where the quill was the primary writing tool and parchment the medium, to imagine a world in which word processors existed. Speculating as much as you like, what do you imagine the writing world will look like in 20 years, 50 years, and 200 years?

In 20 years, I think the writing world will look much like it does now, but we will have come to accept certain creative writing 'products' as AI-generated and/or AI-informed (that is, using LLMs to develop the work). While we will continue to identify the human authors of those works and read the works with the idea that there is a human author behind each one of them, some of those authors will have mostly used AI and AI prompt writing to create those works.

In 50 years, any concern over use of AI in creative writing will long have passed. However, it is my prediction that concern will have morphed into nuances and degrees of choice. AI informed works (and by then AI-generated works) will have become part of a wider range of choices those who buy fiction and poetry (in particular) can make—adding to but not superseding creative writing works where little or no AI is used. In that sense, and though the comparison is connected but somewhat oblique, we might think of the choice today of buying the book or watching the film or playing the game or doing all three! Or of deciding whether to buy an e-book, a paperback or a hardback. The comparisons aren't really close enough to be entirely useful, I know, but the simple thought is that AI will add choice not take away opportunity for creative writers to work in a variety of ways (AI enabled or not).

Looking 200 years into the future is not entirely like looking 200 years into the past, given the often undue confidence created by hindsight. I start thinking of book publishing by subscription, that took place just beyond 200 years in the past. I think of changes that took place back then in the cost of printing books, due to technological advancements, and the increase in books printed and, from that, books being read.

But 200 years hence? I wonder if might be that if we can speak of creative writing today, despite the many changes that have taken place over the past two hundred years, that we will also speak of creative writing in 200 years' time, and ponder the longevity of it then as we ponder its longevity now?

9. If you had all the time you needed, what written work would you like to write and why? It doesn't have to be a work of creative writing. Would you use AI to write it; and, if so, how would you use it?

I would like to write a multi-layered historical novel, an origin story. I would not use AI to help me write it—mostly because I enjoy the work of writing creatively and I don't get the same satisfaction working with Generative AI, not in the doing of it and not in the outcomes of using it.

10. Who benefits most from using AI? Anyone more than anyone else? Any industry more than any other industry? Any place or places in the world? Do you think more people or fewer people might write creatively because of the existence and application of AI—if so, why; if not, why not?

I think those who get access to it, and that will not be everyone, everywhere, will benefit from it. It will help them complete some less enjoyable tasks. The industrial world will benefit more than elsewhere in the world. Wealthier locations, communities and individuals will benefit more than the less wealthy.

Questions of the bias of the material on which Generative AI draws also come to mind, and the uneven aspects of this, the lack of wider representation, the dangers of machines drawing on data that is itself already biased.

In my view, we'll see a shift of participation in creative writing—mostly an opening up of it, as more people feel they can try it, using AI to explore their thoughts, feelings and observations. This is a kind of empowerment. However, we will also see some creative writers become less interested in creative writing, because the experience will be diminished for those writers—and not only those who were already writing before the use of AI became more widespread, but also those who wonder what it is like to create art in writing where each aspect is a combination of your own thoughts, experiences and imagination, and immediate, in that sense, and personal, and fleeting, and meaningful.

References

Motion, Andrew. *Randomly Moving Particles* (Pitt Poetry Series). Kindle Edition. University of Pittsburgh Press.

Schneider, K. J. 2024. Tech-Vexed: The Awesome Price for Artifice. In *Values and Indigenous Psychology in the Age of the Machine and Market*, ed. A. Dueck and L. Sundararajan. Cham: Palgrave Macmillan. https://doi.org/10.1007/978-3-031-53196-5_3.

Michael Dean Clark

Abstract **Michael Dean Clark** says: AI is a powerful tool with the potential to draw on literary, scientific, and cultural references, mirroring human culture if not itself being human. AI's utility is clear, assisting with language refinement, structural modeling and research, but it is not inherently creative. Rather, it is a tool capable of pattern-recognition, devoid of consciousness, imagination, or intent. Human creativity involves failure and is often a slow process. There are dangers in AI—such as found in algorithmic erasure and cultural homogenization. There are benefits too, when AI is used critically and relationally. In these cases, it can be a diagnostic and reflective tool, enhancing human writing, if it is not used merely for commodification and to provide literary shortcuts. Empathy, patience, community, and risk are core to artistic expression, and the positive future for AI and creative writing lies in not reducing such practice to the production of literature-as-content. Careful, equity-minded engagement with AI with attention to questions of process, voice, and the imagination empower human writers in ways that machines, currently, cannot truly achieve.

Keywords Authorship · Imagination · Pattern · Process · Homogenization

G. Harper (ed.), *AI and Creative Writing*,
https://doi.org/10.1007/978-3-031-99101-1_6

Michael Dean Clark is a professor of writing and an author of fiction and literary nonfiction. His academic work is primarily situated in exploring various modes of pedagogy and he is the co-editor of three collections: *Creative Writing in the Digital Age* (2015); *Creative Writing Innovations* (2018), and *Innovative Teaching Through Creative Writing* (2021). Set primarily in San Diego, his creative work has been listed as notable in *Best American Essays* and nominated for Pushcart Prize and Best of the Net consideration. It has appeared in *Pleiades*, *Drunk Monkeys*, *Angel City Review*, *The Other Journal*, *Punctuate*, and T*he Jabberwock Review* among others. He lives, writes, and teaches in Southern California.

1. When someone says 'Artificial Intelligence' what things do you think about?

When the words 'Artificial Intelligence' are uttered, my response is what popular culture and media have trained into me: sentient machines that act as a mirror for viewing human frailty and character. Half panacea and half apocalyptic prophesy in techno-human form. Somewhere between James Spader's Ultron and Haley Joel Osment's David. I guess the humanist in me reads AI like Mary Shelley's *Frankenstein*, a story more about the creator and their culture than the 'monster' they've created.

As a writer, though, AI conjures more specific and participatory models of thinking. Nick Monfort's open-sourced, proto self-iterative poem generator, 'Takoro Gorge' comes to mind, as does its distant technological progeny *I Am Code*, a 2023 collection of poems 'authored' by code-davinci-002. These two endeavors are simultaneously related and disparate in the ways they engage the question of authorship and the connection between humans and machines. In between these two systems, I also think of market-driven platforms like Sudowrite, patterned in its founder's marketing language as human storytellers' 'writing partner.' These platforms offer up suggestions from potential outlines to word choice to wholesale revisions of passages users can see as plug-and-play with the copy/paste functions. All of these are not so much creative products as probability models based on the data sets the service's large language model (LLM) has trained on. What the human half of the partnership does with these suggestions dictates my response to the technology's role.

Central to my associations with AI are the very predictable human impulses to move quickly from considering what is possible with an idea or technology to the wholesale race to inculcate AI in the popular imagination as the next necessity. While it likely is, the complicated ethical, environmental, and, in this context, authorial implications are so often bypassed for the sake of commercial and cultural gain. In essence, AI has equal capacity to simplify and complicate life in ways we are only just beginning to take seriously in any broad sense, hence the earlier reference to science fiction. It seems, as so often is the case, we should be listening to writers when we think about the nature and realities of AI.

2. Thinking of antonyms of 'intelligence', would it be possible, do you think, to have 'Artificial Unintelligence' or 'Artificial Stupidity' or 'Artificial Awkwardness' and, if so, what might they look like?

As a product with its basis in human design and thinking, AI becomes unintelligent when it is assumed to be creative, meaning the lack of intelligence is on the human side of the equation. I don't read AI as smart or unsmart so much as a function of directional processing power. Pointed in a direction with parameters set for human expectation, it simply sifts data at rates no human can comprehend through a simple comparison to their own process. Think: the omniscient figure in Borges's 'Library of Babel.'[1] Whether the returns of that processing are smart are not hinges on the differences between knowledge, intelligence, and wisdom, concepts human artists have explored as long as consciousness and culture have carved out space for such explorations.

So what is Artificial Unintelligence? Programming that has not interrogated itself for biases, limits in perspective, and disregard for ideas outside of the parameters that set it in motion. Intelligence and wisdom carry a meta-criticality that seeks to test ideas against themselves for the sake of ensuring their quality beyond simply seeming 'correct.' Again, this is a human perspective, as machines do not so much think about their 'thinking' as enact it. A great example of this is the oft-cited development of AlphaGo, a program that did the unthinkable (at the time) and beat one of the best Go players in the world in 2016. In a match the human player seemed on the verge of winning, the program flipped the contest's

[1] Borges, Jorge Luis. *The Library of Babel*. Penguin Classics. New York, NY. 25, May 2023.

momentum with a move its competitor had never considered before. The human player went on to lose the match, took only one match in the series (with a surprising move of his own some posit only happened because of what he learned from AlphaGo's unorthodox approach), and retired from the game.

AlphaGo's strategy was indeed surprising. But contrary to some takes on the moment, I'd argue this wasn't a moment of creativity as humans conceive it, a process that often includes moments of epiphanic inspiration outside of humans' conscious understanding of their thoughts. It was one of processing. AlphaGo's move was not so much a stroke of inspired play as an option that existed outside the human player's experience and the human culture surrounding gameplay itself.

I can hear the argument now: but isn't that exactly what art is? The answer is it would be if that were the intent of the machine. But machines do not, at this point, operate on intent. The humans who programmed it did. And this is no mere semantic difference. It is the exact same critical model applied to human products when considering their artistic merit, a participatory model where artist and viewer learn from the inquiry.

As such, I'd define Artificial Unintelligence as the drive to employ the results of AI without human participation and learning. One might argue the cultural drive to replace human art with machine products (see: the core concerns informing the Hollywood writers' strike of 2023) is a prime example of Artificial Unintelligence.

3. What kinds of things can AI help creative writers do? What kind of AI might help them best?

Humans are already cyborgs. Technology has extended our memory, reach, and processing power for centuries. In this way, AI is an extension of that relationship. For creative writers, I'd divide its help into two categories: the assistance being marketed as such by business interests connected with the technology and the less apparent relational benefits of considering what our creation can teach us ourselves.

In the first category, AI's assistance leans toward the mechanical. Language refinement and sample expressions of ideas a writer is considering become readily available algorithmic suggestions. When researching, writers can use AI to synthesize mountains of content on a subject they need to present accurately for a line or scene to function as intended. And in some cases, a refined inquiry will lead to AI offering writers insights into their content they may not otherwise have seen (as a simple example, think of applying a word cloud generator to a manuscript and discovering which terms are employed most to recognize themes in the writer's language choices). There are, of course, proponents of AI's creative capacity that see its products as approaching human levels of creativity, but I do not subscribe to this conclusion for reasons elaborated on elsewhere.

What I am most interested in, as a writer and someone who helps other humans take ownership of their process, is how AI might help us learn ourselves in more refined terms. This is a framework for which I owe a debt to N. Katherine Hayles's *Writing Machines* and *How We Became Posthuman*. In those books, the notion of technology as a departure from human agency is contested with a view of a relational continuum in which writing must be viewed as what it has been is stitched into what it is becoming in the contexts of various technologies. In essence, every generation uses expression based on what has come before it to wield language in a way that makes sense of their present tense, language that folds back into the next generation's attempt to do the same.

There are many ways I see this being possible if AI is considered another way for humans to learn these lessons, but I'll trace one taken from Marcus Du Sautoy's excellent book *The Creativity Code*.[2] To highlight human-AI partnerships' potential for giving humans new language to apply to their writing process, he traced composer David Cope's attempts to develop an algorithm capable of writing compositions rivaling those of revered composers, most centrally Bach. While the musical product of Cope's work is fascinating, what caught my attention most was how the process ended up developing new language now widely used by other composers. This language—a product of the algorithm's study of patterns in existing classical compositions and Cope's analysis of its results—helped human composers reshape their understanding of both their own writing and that of other composers.

The possibilities of this kind of learning for human writers—lessons that address the relationship of human intention and process into starker relief—are infinitely more exciting to me than any mechanical assistance AI can offer.

[2] Du Sautoy, Marcus. *The Creativity Code: Art and Innovation in the Age of AI*. The Bellknap Press of Harvard. Cambridge, MA. 2019. (pp. 183-190).

4. What things can AI not help creative writers do? (and this could be specifically associated with their writing or more generally in their lives)

When ChatGPT's presence was first splashily announced, I turned to Twitter and wrote a long thread on my immediate concerns regarding its potential impact on human writers like the ones in my classrooms. At the core of those worries is its inability to teach the kind of patience writing creatively requires. I thought, immediately of a note in Anne LaMott's *Bird by Bird*, in which she recounts 'I heard a preacher say recently that hope is a revolutionary patience; let me add that so is being a writer. Hope begins in the dark, stubborn hope that if you just show up and try to do the right thing, the dawn will come. You wait and watch and work: you don't give up.'[3] The most difficult and rewarding element of the human creative writing process is the painful wait that comes with seeking the best expression of our ideas, Flaubert's 'le mot juste.' This process has no established map, no protocol to be applied to all situations equally, and as humans are not simply processing machines like AI, we must learn to manage the frustration necessary for creative expression to develop.

In a related sense, AI cannot teach writers the importance of outliers and 'mistakes' in its current form. As a probability refining system, it has little to say to passive users on the necessity of failure as its process for returning results to inquiries is a black box to anyone without a computer science degree and specific set of experiences with the technology. Given that humans often see the specifics of their own process as shrouded, the way AI generates responses can act as a disincentive to writers digging in and finding the language necessary to understand their own needs in various writing situations.

Also, AI does not seem to have a sense of the implications of its words beyond the parameters of its programming, coding often ignorant of the impositions of its programmers' perspectives and blind spots. This is a recipe for erasure, of marginalized voices and expressions that fall outside of the experience set of AI's creators and lacking meta-critical thought on these limitations. In the best circumstances, this is exactly what creative writing teaches those who participate in the process of creating it: the

[3] Lamott, Anne. *Bird by Bird*. Vintage. New York, NY. 1 September 1995.

necessity of working to learn how to pay attention to what is otherwise not obvious to the writer.

In that sense, I find myself wrestling with ways I see AI being unable to teach human writers the necessity of community in their writing. Despite the myth of the author as the solitary genius translating the product of their insights via a particular gifting, the best stories are the result of many human interactions with writers' ideas. At this point, I'd argue the only way one might interpret AI as capable of replacing humans in writers' processes is erroneously reading the term 'writing' as the written product and not the process in its totality. In this way, AI cannot help teach writers to develop the human relationships they'll need to get the most out of their work.

5. If you knew a novel, or a poem or a screenplay was written using AI would it make any difference to how you responded to it as a reader or audience? Does the form of writing make any difference to your response—so, for example, if you knew a film you were watching had a script written using AI or, alternatively, if you were reading a novel written using AI? Does genre make any difference—for example, if you were reading a sonnet or an elegy, or if you were reading a science fiction short story, or if you were reading a video game script for an adventure game?

It does make a difference based on my orientation to literature as an artform rooted in human exchange. I marvel at the moments when authors show me something I would not otherwise have seen. Alice Walker's *The Color Purple* absolutely shattered a 15-year-old me with what is required of the human soul to survive such pain. Katie Ford's poem 'Psalm 40' depicts a fragile moment of hope appearing beyond consuming loss that I cling to. Eula Biss' essay 'The Pain Scale' upended my notion of subjectivity and expression. These are all beautifully written pieces of literature, but the reason they resonate is not simply their authors' technical proficiency or craft mastery. It is knowing I am reading something another human felt compelled to wrestle out of themselves, something that required risk, something that cost the author. These are not merely collections of words, but invitations into a moment of human connection. That a human is extending the invitation, whether I like the work or not, matters to me.

Another reason the human authorship of a work matters to me is the growing conflation of content with art. In his book *Everything and Less*,[4] historian Mark McGurl traces the intersections between literature and the digital marketplace of Amazon. As the largest distributor of literature in the world and a publisher platforming an ever-increasing number of self-published works on its own Kindle network, McGurl posits that the nature the novel and Amazon itself have become increasingly entangled in connected human desires for comfort and instant gratification. Novels, then, are simply consumer goods middle class buyers purchase in orders also containing new shirts, vitamins, and toilet paper. In the 'everything store' as McGurl calls it, every element in this process from the author's identity to the work they attach their name to becomes a product, moving creativity into simply a profit-loss relationship focused almost entirely on fulfilling readers need for comfort on demand.

In this literature-as-content model, algorithmic story engines with adept humans guiding them are well suited to write novels increasingly dialed into expressed human desires for comfort at speeds no human can match. But art is not about speed and often seeks to discomfort when the reader's comfort is violence or erasure for others. In some cases, this discomfort only makes sense because of the way the author has experienced it and then prismed their feelings onto the page or screen via the particularity of those experiences. At this point, machines cannot mimic that process, just its products.

So, as an object of study, I am interested in what AI can produce as a recapitulation of human work. AI has the ability to help me see human work differently and, maybe, better by decontextualizing the structures it is reproducing from their origins. But I am also cognizant that its creation is the result of a machine sifting existing human expression more than trying to express something it thinks the reader needs to be brought in contact with in an original context. Even in a blind reading test, being fooled by the algorithm is not so much proof that machine expression is on par with that of humans (though, it will make fewer technical errors in the process than even excellent human writers). What it represents is more likely the way our expectations of art are being changed by the market.

[4] McGurl, Mark. *Everything and Less: The Novel in the Age of Amazon*. Verso. London, UK. 2021.

6. Does any AI have imagination? If so, in way or ways? It not, why not? Do you believe it could ever have imagination?

As noted earlier, AI is built on large-scale pattern recognition and probability models. It performs an ever-refining search for the most normatively appropriate responses given the parameters of the inquiry it is processing. In essence, it crunches massive amounts of data looking for consensus. This is extremely useful in, say, distilling the myriad studies of pharmaceutical side-effects for a particular series of cancer treatments or trends in house prices over time. But calling pattern recognition in the review of others' words the equivalent of imagination is a misread in my opinion.

As such, I'd say AI has does not possess imagination—yet. Could it develop one? Maybe. But my question is this: if humans come wired with imagination as a central need and processing system—something required for our survival—what will machines need to achieve that same innateness? Emotions? A sense of self in relation to their surroundings? A desire to better understand both of those elements? If these questions sound familiar, it's because almost every depiction of AI in science fiction centers on them, which in turn reveals these to be intensely human concerns enacted on the technological 'other' for which the imagination is vital.

At the point that AI achieves this level of self-awareness and an ingrained sense that it is exploring mysteries beyond its ability to articulate in the present moment, mysteries it self-identifies as such and 'feels' compelled to find language for, then I'd say it has achieved imagination.

7. The previous question touched on the notion of whether AI can itself be imaginative. The follow up, then, is whether it can (itself) form new ideas, have sensations, form memories? Can AI actually think? Can it feel?

I don't believe so. In much the same way humans apply anthropomorphic renderings of animals in animated films, we also extend our sense of identity and cognizance to machines. Interestingly, those fictional human machines and animals all seem to suffer from the same frailties and cruelties humans do. It's almost as if we are writing a narrative of ourselves using safer others as stand-ins that allow us to feel justified in the belief that we have evolved beyond them.

In my estimation, AI becomes sentient in ways humans recognize only if techno-futurists predictions of the convergence of human and digital processing come to pass. And then, we will be discussing something altogether different, a hybrid notion of existence that we really still barely have language to approach in terms of understanding. Apologies to Kurzweil and the rest, but simply finding a way to make this merger happen does not constitute understanding its implications, let alone the experience of it.

This, I would say, is a powerful argument supporting our absolute need to slow down and wrestle out where we are now in the way the creative process demands. Our stories and poems are the messy and fraught process through which we stumble toward understanding. They contend with political and personal powers and frailties that, if left unexplored in ways that transgress and interrogate the norms of the powerful few, foster tribalism and erasure at the margins. In this way, careful application of what AI does well could absolutely lead humans to greater understandings of their own process, which would feed back into AI's development of its own capacities in those spaces.

But can it feel or think: not in the ways we define. Maybe the first lesson it could teach humans is that we need to stop trying to define machine intelligence and creative capacity solely in human or machine terms, but in the relational sense our shared work presents us.

8. It might have been impossible for someone from the medieval period, where the quill was the primary writing tool and parchment the medium, to imagine a world in which word processors existed. Speculating as much as you like, what do you imagine the writing world will look like in 20 years, 50 years, and 200 years?

When it comes to the intrinsic humanistic purposes of writing, I look to social media as a model of where the practice will go. In most cases, we will 'write' about ourselves more but continue to remain mysteries to ourselves on this trajectory. This has always been the case in the sense that writing creatively, as it is conceived in terms of a focused development of storytelling norms and craft considerations, has been more of a niche process than a norm for the majority of humans. And this is sad, because the human capacity for imaginative creation is vast. But the cultural value of employing that creativity in service of anything outside of financial accumulation limits where writing liberates.

In an interactive framework then, AI has the capacity to open more windows on creativity if users read it like they would a human artist. In a

2012 interview,[5] author Dave Eggers claimed one of his models for great sentences has been Saul Bellow. 'Not that my sentences look much like his' he said quickly. This, I think, is a model for the kind of reading that makes AI most useful to human writers. When writers analyze the work of others, the ideas they gather don't generally lead to strict imitation. Rather, they expand our ideas of what is possible in our own explorations of style and expression, which expands our ability to create the kinds of relationships with readers creative works are capable of. AI analysis and imitation of a vast array of styles in quick order could be a boon to writers seeking to understand themselves in reflection.

Unfortunately, I see an equally plausible possibility in the use of increasingly nuanced image filters like those seen on social media platforms. As AI-enabled writing systems increase in sophistication, more people will be able to present themselves as authors. As NVIDIA CEO Jensen Huang said, 'AI will come for the fiction writers first.'[6] But how will we be able to trust the stories we find are anything more than literary face-tuning technology? And what will that do to notions of relationships and isolation?

Given the way AI seeks the most probable response to any inquiry, the thing I fear most is the inevitable increase in cultural homogeneity that will come as a result. And, as humans tend to be bias-confirmation seeking in nature, that homogeneity becomes antithetical to the aims of art as a resistance to simply ceding creative acts to those with the most control of cultural production. Art diversifies through resistance. Through difference. Through dissent. All of those responses require a heterodox reading of culture that seeks outliers as necessary to expression. As always, for me, this leads back to the reality that potential is solely rooted in human response to opportunity, something that is absolutely true for the future of writing.

9. If you had all the time you needed, what written work would you like to write and why? It doesn't have to be a work of creative writing. Would you use AI to write it; and, if so, how would you use it?

[5] Eggers, Dave. Interview. *Writer's Symposium by the Sea*. San Diego, CA. 1 March 2012.

[6] Witt, Stephen. "How Jensen Huang's NVDIA Is Powering the A.I. Revolution." *The New Yorker*. 27 November 2023. Accessed: https://www.newyorker.com/magazine/2023/12/04/how-jensen-huangs-nvidia-is-powering-the-ai-revolution.

My reasons for writing are quite analog, as people my age would say in relation to technology. I simply want to write stories that cost me something to create, a cost I see as an investment in what people who read them will get from my efforts. And as cautious as I am about touting the potentials of AI, I do see several ways that AI can help me achieve those goals. In long form, my ideas tend toward multi-voice narrative and novels in stories.

For example, my Melvillian white whale is a twelve-voice novel that centers around a shared traumatic event and told at various levels of remove from the event itself. Steeped in a number of other overlays, to call the story complicated is an understatement, and I've been looking for a way to tell it for more than a decade. I see numerous ways I could use AI to help model and nuance the connections between the character narratives for narrative cohesion. It could create visual maps of relationships via direct connections in the text. It could read my text for tone and give me heat maps for various forms of expression I'm using and how often they appear. It could extend my research at moments when a particular detail is needed but not at hand via refined search parameters, allowing for quicker access to the ideas I'm searching for. It could even scan my manuscript for timeline continuities and offer setting suggestions with properly worded queries. In short, it could help me see my story from a variety of angles that could unlock elements that have left me, to date, stumped.

This is basically my philosophy in terms of using AI. If it is diagnostic; if it helps writers see their process and its products more clearly so they can return to them better equipped to achieve their vision, then it is a net benefit. But that is a relational model of interaction with technology, a meta-cognitive dialogue that requires more effort on the part of the writer, not less. And this is in contrast to the dominant framing of AI as making work 'easier' and the worker's life 'better' as a result.

10. Who benefits most from using AI? Anyone more than anyone else? Any industry more than any other industry? Any place or places in the world? Do you think more people or fewer people might write creatively because of the existence and application of AI—if so, why; if not, why not?

The response is in the question itself: industries in countries that monopolize natural resources benefit most from AI, regardless of what economic sector they serve. Technology is extremely powerful, but access and the knowledge of how to apply it act as gatekeeping mechanisms. To bluntly, AI is only useful when people are given the space and tools to use it.

There are vast possible benefits to the individual writer when it comes to using AI. Instant access to models for their own writing. Increasingly nuanced translations for texts from other cultures and language traditions, though, as any translator will tell you, the nuance and quality of those translations may be questionable given machine's propensities to aim for the middle of meaning. The power to research across massive amounts of data in ways unimaginable to a majority of humans even in my lifetime. In a broader sense, AI could become what people predicted the computer would be from its inception, the implement that freed humans from labor machines could perform in their stead, freeing them up to be more focused on creativity.

But potential benefits must be weighed against actual and eventual application. Proponents of AI development often frame it as 'democratizing creativity' and, I suppose, there are lenses that allow for that interpretation. However, commercial interests control access, and that model always benefits the shareholder more than artists. When I look at how AI is being marketed to writers in particular, this is clearly a dynamic at play given the best uses of AI are likely not writing stories and poems, yet moving AI into those human processes has received a great deal of focus and effort on the part of industry. It begs the question: why? If AI art is simply being positioned as the next profit-driver, the division between who can and cannot benefit from it will increase. To achieve the vast potential AI holds for individuals, access to it must be democratized via the technology itself and the education surrounding not just how to use it but also the implications of doing so.

Katy Ilonko Gero

Abstract **Katy Ilonko Gero** says: the term 'artificial intelligence' is a catch-all term that lacks precision while offering cultural utility in referencing large language models (LLMs) and generative tools. Different writers adopt AI in diverse, often unpredictable ways—regularly employing it in idea generation or in drafting. Others find AI tools creatively stifling. Rather than pondering whether AI can 'think' or 'feel' it is more productive to approach computational systems on their own terms, not using such a human experiential analogy. AI cannot truly author or imagine in a human sense, though it might be said to offer combinatorial and exploratory creativity. The relationship between AI and creative writing also raises ethical and economic questions around attribution and compensation for human authors, and there is risk of homogenization in creative outputs. AI can coexist with human-authored works, much as photography has complemented painting. It is essentially a tool, shaped by and embedded in human intention and infrastructure. Most important is our careful engagement in AI's promise as well as in the inequities in AI's role in creative practice.

Keywords Authorship · Poetry · Creativity · Thesaurus · Labor

G. Harper (ed.), *AI and Creative Writing*,
https://doi.org/10.1007/978-3-031-99101-1_7

Katy Ilonka Gero Is a human-computer interaction researcher, with a focus on creativity and writing assistants. Her PhD thesis focused on how creative writers make use of language models, but recently she has become more interested in the ethics of data collection, how to create and support community models (i.e., models created outside of and in resistance to corporate models), and the impact of computer-generated text on ownership, authorship, and learning. She is currently a Postdoctoral Fellow in Computer Science at Harvard University, as well as a Fellow with the Library Innovation Lab, housed in the Harvard Law Library. Her research has been supported by a National Science Foundation Graduate Research Fellowship, the Brown Institute for Media Innovation, and an Amazon Research Award. In addition to her research, she is a poet and essayist, with work published in *Wired, Catapult*, *the HTML Review,* and more. She was a Writer in Residence at the Vermont Studio Center in 2022, and was on the editorial board for *taper*, a literary magazine for small computational pieces, from 2022–2023. Along with Kyle Booten, Katy recently founded *Ensemble Park*, a literary magazine that collects experiments in human-computer co-writing. Her first book of poetry, *The Anxiety of Conception* (Nothing to Say Press, 2025), will be released next year. In 2025, she will join the faculty in the School of Computer Science at the University of Sydney.

1. When someone says 'Artificial Intelligence' what things do you think about?

I have a conflicted relationship with the term 'Artificial Intelligence'. On one hand, I think it is used to describe all kinds of different technologies, making it useless as a descriptor of any distinguishing feature of a given technology other than, perhaps, recency. (The interesting term 'Good Old-Fashioned AI' describes symbolic AI, which was popular in the 1960s and remains influential and useful in certain contexts today.) These days, people often mean deep neural networks, though even that encompasses a broad range of technologies. A statistics professor I had in graduate school used to tell the joke that when you're talking to investors, you call it 'artificial intelligence', when you're recruiting software developers you called it 'neural networks', and when you go to actually build the thing you call it 'logistic regression'. So as a Computer Scientist I find it to be a frustrating term. On the other hand, it is term which people use to describe current influential technologies that have some relationship to human intelligence, and I cannot ignore its utility as a shorthand, right now, for large language models, text-to-image generators, high-performance classifiers, and large neural models more broadly.

2. Thinking of antonyms of 'intelligence', would it be possible, do you think, to have 'Artificial Unintelligence' or 'Artificial Stupidity' or 'Artificial Awkwardness' and, if so, what might they look like?

Absolutely. In fact, if we think of large language models as an example, I think it's reasonable to argue that they have both artificial intelligence and artificial stupidity. Large language models struggle with things that humans, and in fact other kinds of artificial intelligence (I'm thinking now of symbolic AI mentioned above,) find quite trivial, like keeping track of small numbers of objects, or solving puzzles like wordle or sudoku. I think it's useful to consider the 'intelligence' of something like a large language model as something distinct from human intelligence, rather than a poor facsimile of such. In the same way that a calculator can handily outperform people in performing large arithmetic operations but we would not expect to be able to converse with us, we should expect that the capabilities and limits of large language models do not neatly map onto our own.

3. What kinds of things can AI help creative writers do? What kind of AI might help them best?

Oof, this is a contentious question. Writers of different stripes will, and are, finding AI helpful in different ways. I have heard of writers using AI to suggest plotlines, help develop characters, keep track of complicated world dynamics, get through writer's block by suggesting next sentences or paragraphs, draft whole chapters, give feedback on drafts, add description to a scene, act as an AI character in a story, suggest word replacements in poetry, title a story or poem, and more. (We can also consider activities outside of the writing itself--writing blurbs, marketing materials, etc.) I expect that creative writers will make use of AI in ways I cannot even dream of. In fact, in a study I did with Kyle Booten a few years back (Booten et al.), we asked poets to dream up a hypothetical 'poetry machine' that could perform some custom, computational operation for them, and the results were both diverse and surprising to us. This is what people do–-in the face of new technologies (and I use the term technology here very broadly) we will invariably do strange and wonderful things with it.

However, for each of these use cases, there will be writers who believe AI is *not* useful for such a thing. For instance, I have interviewed numerous writers who say that AI is not useful for any of the things listed above: they have tried these things and have found AI lacking. It is an interesting research question to me to understand what makes some writers so amenable to what AI can currently do, and other writers critical. An initial theory is that older writers are less open to such technologies, but I would offer that it is less age than experience as a writer; older writers who have just begun their writing journey can be, in my experience, very open to AI support. But this does not explain all the variation I have seen.

As for the second part of the question, I do think the current trend of large language models is pushing them towards banality, because the more common use case of these models is not in a creative context. Thus, I think models that are less obsequious and more weird will be most useful for writers.

4. What things can AI not help creative writers do? (and this could be specifically associated with their writing or more generally in their lives)

I am going to return to my proposition that this is a contentious question. I think perhaps the problem is talking about creative writers as a monolith, whereas the nature of creativity in writing is that writers are not repeating the same act as writers before them. Not getting too deep into the philosophy of writing, of which I am certainly not an expert, some writers are excellent stylists, others produce compelling plots, etc. It makes sense that a writer who prides themselves on the prosody of their sentences is less interested in computational support for drafting their words; however a writer focused on intricate plots may take less issue with computational support for the prosody of their work. I see this as a testament to the rich nature of writing–-it is not just about beautiful sentences, or complicated plot, or dynamic characters, or anything else it. Writing is such a multitude of different things that any one writer needn't feel their humanity is tied up in every single little piece.

Which is all to say that AI is not helpful for just about everything it is helpful for.

I personally have not found AI to be particularly helpful in my writing practice, with the exception of a set of computational generated thesauruses I created several years ago (Gero and Chilton). I think this says as much about me and my interests as a writer than the capabilities of AI.

5. If you knew a novel, or a poem or a screenplay was written using AI would it make any difference to how you responded to it as a reader or audience? Does the form of writing make any difference to your response—so, for example, if you knew a film you were watching had a script written using AI or, alternatively, if you were reading a novel written using AI? Does genre make any difference—for example, if you were reading a sonnet or an elegy, or if you were reading a science fiction short story, or if you were reading a video game script for an adventure game?

Absolutely. Of course AI can encompass such a broad range of technologies. Spell-check, at one point, would have been considered AI; now I would not bat an eye to learn that a book had used an automatic spell-checker. This is not to suggest that the AI of today is not something fundamentally different to spell-check, but only to say that cultural norms can shift unexpectedly.

Still, as a reader or an audience, as well as an artist, I consider art to be a communicative practice between people. Computational intervention in this practice does not forbid the human-to-human connection. And this may be the moment to point out that I don't believe AI could ever create something without any human involvement; AI does not have any goals or intent that are not in some way provided by a person. To say something is 'authored' by an AI is, in my opinion, untrue. AI cannot be an author. (I believe the US Copyright Office agrees with me.) Instead, when people claim that something is created 'by an AI', I think they mean that there was far less human involvement than expected. This is not the same thing, though, and the distinction is important to me because saying a novel or script or poem has an AI author perpetuates a misunderstanding of how technology works.

But to return to my point, yes, I care about the involvement of AI in the creative process. Because I am so familiar with how the technology works, I am always intensely curious about the details of how the AI was created and how it was used. This doesn't mean I wouldn't enjoy a novel or poem or screenplay. But in the same way that knowing something about the historical context of a novel, knowing about the meter of a poem, knowing about the motivations of the screenplay studio sponsor, knowing about the author can add (or detract) from the experience of a work of art, so too we should expect AI involvement to shade our experience.

6. Does any AI have imagination**? If so, in way or ways? It not, why not? Do you believe it could ever have imagination?**

No. This is because AI is not a human, and it's hard to know what it means for non-humans to have imagination. But we could reframe this question to ask if AI can come up with ideas that it has not been previously exposed to. Now we can draw on a long line of research into computational creativity, which has explored the abilities of machines to generate new ideas. In particular Margaret Boden's theorizing in this space is useful (Boden, 23). She proposes three types of creativity: combinatorial, exploratory, and transformative. Without going too deep, computers are quite capable of combinatorial creativity, where many combinations of existing ideas can be tested and selected to create new ones. They are also capable of exploring a well-defined 'space' and finding new areas of interest. It is less clear if computers are capable of transformative creativity, where rules are broken and new kinds of ideas are presented, though work on genetic algorithms have demonstrated some success.

7. The previous question touched on the notion of whether AI can itself be imaginative. The follow up, then, is whether it can (itself) form new ideas, have sensations, form memories? Can AI actually think? Can it feel?

I've already addressed the question about new ideas. Sensations, memories, thinking, and feeling are quite different. Let's imagine a small, simple computer that sits outside. It has sensors that provide an incoming stream of information about, say, the amount of light hitting its box and the moisture in the air. Not only is there an incoming stream of data, it also records a history of the light and moisture, perhaps over years. Maybe, even, it has a finite storage capacity, and so remembers certain moments of light and moisture readings more 'clearly' than others--like a moment when it was raining very heavily and yet the sun was out. It then uses this stream of information and stored past information to write poetry. Would we say that such an 'AI' is having sensations and forming memories? I propose that instead of distorting a computational system by mapping it one-to-one to our own experiential framework, we instead let such a system have its own kind of intelligence. Going back to our small computer outside, it is writing poetry using a history of light and moisture readings. Is it 'thinking' about these when writing? I'm not sure I really care. Instead, I would ask, 'How is it making use of that data? How is it writing poetry?'

8. It might have been impossible for someone from the medieval period, where the quill was the primary writing tool and parchment the medium, to imagine a world in which word processors existed. Speculating as much as you like, what do you imagine the writing world will look like in 20 years, 50 years, 200 years?

In 50 years, I expect there will be computationally generated books, perhaps generated to order. Perhaps you'd like a book that is loosely based on your own life, or a book that imagines your dog living on Mars, or any other specific interest of yours. Perhaps you generate a book that you gift to your partner; it in fact is being used as a marriage proposal. You will not need to be a skilled writer, though perhaps you have some other skill, or perhaps you employee someone with such skills. Such books will exist alongside books as I have experienced them for my life: books written by people for people, perhaps even written longhand before being typed up on a computer. In the same way that photography did not displace painting, I don't expect computer generated literature to displace human written books.

I do hope that human written books, however they are used to contribute to computer generated text, provide compensation to their human authors, perhaps in a way similar to how the Canadian library system compensates authors. Recent work has demonstrated that AI systems trained on their own outputs will devolve (Shumailov, 755–759). The correct valuing of primarily human-authored texts is incredibly important, both for writers and those interested in the abilities of AI; this is something I am actively doing research into.

9. If you had all the time you needed, what written work would you like to write and why? It doesn't have to be a work of creative writing. Would you use AI to write it; and, if so, how would you use it?

There are all kinds of things I would like to work on. I'd like to write another book of poetry; write a novel; do an oral history with my parents; create more mixed-media poetry and digital media poetry. As I mentioned earlier, I am not too interested in AI for the writing process, except as a kind of souped up and wild thesaurus.

10. Who benefits most from using AI? Anyone more than anyone else? Any industry more than any other industry? Any place or places in the world? Do you think more people or fewer people might write creatively because of the existence and application of AI—if so, why; if not, why not?

Our current technological landscape has all the failings of our world more generally: uneven access, profit flowing to a small cohort, building on the labor of uncompensated workers. So this question is tied up in larger questions about who benefits most from AI more generally. Still, yes, I do think more people will write creatively because of AI, in the same way that Instagram and camera technology pulled more people into the fold of photography. It will become easier to create text according to specifications, and that will empower people who otherwise struggle to find their words.

References

Boden, Margaret A. 2009. Computer Models of Creativity. *AI Magazine* 30:3.

Booten, Kyle, and Katy Ilonka Gero. 2021. Poetry Machines: Eliciting Designs for Interactive Writing Tools from Poets. In *Proceedings of the 13th Conference on Creativity and Cognition.*

Gero, Katy Ilonka, and Lydia B. Chilton. 2019. How a Stylistic, Machine-Generated Thesaurus Impacts a Writer's Process. In *Proceedings of the 2019 Conference on Creativity and Cognition.*

Shumailov, Ilia, et al. 2024. AI Models Collapse When Trained on Recursively Generated Data. *Nature* 631: 8022.

Craig Jordan-Baker

Abstract Craig Jordan-Baker says: AI's involvement with creative writing can be viewed through the dual lens of technological reality and cultural imagination. There is a gap between what AI is and what it can become as technological 'imaginaries' shape, design, and impact cultural expectations, guiding innovation as much as the technology itself. Natural language models can be helpful tools for research, dialogue modeling, redrafting, and ideation. Nevertheless, they cannot replace the subjective pleasures and nuanced reflections found in the pursuit of creative writing. Historical parallels, such as those of photography versus painting, show how AI has the ability to transform literary production, especially in formulaic genre—but it will displace human authorship entirely. Play, hybridity, and adaptation are essential future responses to AI in creative writing—and ethical and social questions are pressing. For example, who gets to use AI? Who is excluded? Will AI exacerbate inequity or democratize access to creativity. More inclusive imaginaries grounded in cautious optimism and historical perspective are necessary. Ultimately, it is possible to envision a writing culture where AI coexists with human expression, encouraging new forms of literature than blend computational support with human insight, curiosity, and experimentation.

Keywords Imaginaries · Subjectivity · Tagteam · Formula · Play

G. Harper (ed.), *AI and Creative Writing*,
https://doi.org/10.1007/978-3-031-99101-1_8

Craig Jordan-Baker Is a Senior Lecturer in Creative Writing at the University of Brighton, UK. His research interests include the literary representation of landscape, nature writing, Irish literature, and creative writing theory. During his writing career, Craig has worked on artistic commissions from a variety of publish bodies, such as the National Archives, The Booth Museum of Natural History and The New Forest National Park. As well as having published peer-reviewed research, short stories, arts journalism, and reviews, he has published several books, including the novel *The Nacullians* (2020), a non-fiction work *If the River is Hidden* (2022) and the co-edited collection *Writing Landscape and Setting in the Anthropocene—Britain and Beyond* (2024). His latest novel, *Brick Dust* was published in 2025.

1. When someone says 'Artificial Intelligence' what things do you think about?

I think about two things. One is the Terminator-style apocalypse with dead-eyed AI killer robots ranging about the burnt wastes of the south of England, targeting the few remaining humans who have managed to survive due to luck, wit or the ability to live in very very tight spaces.

The other thing I think about are the systems which are designed to solve problems with high a degree of independence, most obviously (for me) ones that respond to natural language inputs. I think it's important to put these two ideas side by side, because they represent technology on the one hand, and our imaginaries of technology on the other. As a writer interested in intellectual history and technology, my concern is really around how the one (the technology) relates to and structures the other (the imaginaries of technology) and visa versa.

One aspect of this is that often technologies affect technological imaginaries through their *potential* rather than the actual state of that technology in a given moment. So, a very early chat program which can only respond in clumsy and semi-relevant ways to our queries and comments can still have a massive impact on our imaginaries, as it gives us a reason to think about what it would be like if the chatbot could, say, convince us to invest our savings in a bitcoin wallet owned by said chatbot, with the promise of fabulous returns, naturally.

And of course the imaginaries can kick back onto the technology. The 'robber-bot' I suggested above may well be designed because someone has engaged with the imaginaries and then wondered how the technology in its current state might move towards the 'robber-bot', the video call, the teleporter, the computer simulation, the instant message (note that we dropped the 'instant' now).

So I think of two things when someone says 'Artificial Intelligence': The technology as it is, and the wild things we think the technology might be.

2. Thinking of antonyms of 'intelligence', would it be possible, do you think, to have 'Artificial Unintelligence' or 'Artificial Stupidity' or 'Artificial Awkwardness' and, if so, what might they look like?

We do have artificial unintelligence! AI is out there and operating sub-optimally in so many corners of the world, at least in the sense that AI systems often do not do what we want them to do, though I suspect they all do what they were programmed to do. The example I always remember the story of Dr Louise Selby, who due to her 'Dr' title, was refused entry into the women's changing room at her local gym, because the system in place assumed that 'Dr' referred to a male, and males were not allowed in the female changing room. When she complained to the humans running the gym, they found out that said the system could not be changed. Dr Selby was told that she should just drop her 'Dr' title and be satisfied with 'Miss/Mrs/Ms'.

The apparent reason for this was that the AI system was trained on the wrong data, or at least on insufficient, biased or skewed data. The system was working as programmed, but it was not doing what us humans wanted, unless there really was a patriarchal plot to make women feel less important. In this case, it seemed to have worked perfectly!

In AI terms, this is already something of an old story, but it's a useful one because it allows us to see the distinction between design intent and programming. It seems to me no use for a programmer to complain that an AI was not doing what it was programed to do. What, other than rely on its programming, can an AI do? Nothing. In strict sense, the problem comes between the design intent and the extent to which the program is a reflection of that intent. This also allows us to see the ways in which our imaginaries might be less exciting and extreme than the ways AI goes wrong or acts unintelligently/stupidly/awkwardly in practice.

However, if we take the intent/programming distinction, another possibility sidles into view: a system that is intentionally designed to be broken, inefficient or have a tendency to produce errors. It's a little like a master watchmaker who deliberately makes a watch which runs to 61 seconds per minute. In such a case, the intent and the programming are in harmony, though we might not think this if we are trying to accurately tell the time (which is a characteristic activity of looking at a watch or timepiece). So there's a question for me about why we might do this, because so many of our AI systems have, do and will act in unintelligent/stupid/awkward ways in the future.

3. What kinds of things can AI help creative writers do? What kind of AI might help them best?

I think most of the ways in which AI might help writers is through AI systems that use natural language, rather than systems like AlphaFold, say, which model the folding of proteins in the brain to better understand neurological degenerative disorders (though this might help a few of us in due course!).

The first way is already well known, and it's the way many non-writer users engage with AI: A research conversation. Unlike using a web for answers, Chatbots have more context-dependent responses so whether you are researching milkfloats or your Welsh ancestry, the programmed remembers information already given and you can refer to that. It's much easier to build on research rather than scanning a linear plane, as you do with a standard engine search. And the ability to have multiple conversations also offers you the opportunity to integrate them.

Another tool which is in the same broad vein is dialogue. Chatbots are a good tool to help writers model dialogue for a play, novel, film, etc., The fact the system can understand the context, respond accordingly and deliver credible (if unscintillating) dialogue that keeps the conversation going and is sensitive to social context of the scene is really impressive, and in some cases beyond what some of my students are capable of.

And the list really could go on: proofing, mind-mapping, suggesting solutions to plot problems, redrafting along any number of parameters, etc., etc. Perhaps the answer to the question is 'everything', including giving you more time to write by filling out your shopping list and then placing your bulk orders of coffee and quick-cook ramen.

And as I'm writing this, I'm thinking, should I have used AI to help me write this? Would it have done a faster job? A better job? At the moment, I'm resistant to do doing, but I imagine that in 10 years' time I'll be far less resistant. To some this prospect of change might seem unsettling, and it is, but that change is already happening, and so are tools for dealing with that change, I'm more interested than concerned.

4. What things can AI not help creative writers do? (and this could be specifically associated with their writing or more generally in their lives)

Something AI would not be able to replace is the pleasure of thinking for yourself within your own active and attentive subjectivity. Indeed, I don't think it would aim to replace anything so abstract and unpractical, because such reflection is the very definition of 'idle' and 'pointless' that a highly commercialized, anti-intellectual and product-orientated society would abhor. But that pleasure of mulling over a sentence, a word choice, the motivations of a character whose entire substance is—at one point—only in the writer's mind is something resistant to the rise of AI and indeed, for that reason, might come to take on a particular value in some corners of society. This is not a quality reserved just for writers, though I think such reflection is slightly more prevalent in writing than is other activities.

And then as well as this, there are things that AI cannot help us do right now. AI is still pretty bad at tube directions, it can't make a decent jacket potato, and for me at least, its attempts at dialogue are passable and largely reactive (but still very impressive considering).

I suppose the question here might be answered by a tub-thumping appeal to the irrepressible spirit of the human, but I'm suspicious of that stance for two reasons. One is that we struggle to predict the future and the impact of technology, which is one of the reasons we have imaginaries of technologies. These imaginaries are themselves though only the roughest of rough guides, as they are often geared towards sensationalism or a need to reflect the problems of our society now, rather than our society in the future. As I've already said, I'm a fan of our imaginaries of technology, but I'm no diehard fan of them, and the Imaginaries of Technology have produced quite a few sub-par albums.

The other reason I'm suspicious of the 'irrepressible humanity' line is that intellectual history is full of examples where we humans try to reserve a quality or qualities for ourselves that are 'essentially' human, and this project fails. In the Classical period and beyond, we had the idea of the 'natural slave' who lacked some quality of soul to make them fully human. We've also used the idea of 'soul' to distinguish us from the animal (as Descartes did). And then we've had the capacity of language as a marker of the human, though we've come to see that some primates can master sign language and some cetaceans appear to use proper names for individuals in their communities. Same goes for tool use and tool making. I've also heard that our ability for suicide or casual sex are also such markers, but what I think we've seen is a failure to find the 'X' factor that will once and for all protect the category of the human.

So overall I don't think we can set a hard boundary about what AI can and cannot do for writers, or for anyone else. Though what we can see perhaps more clearly in the face of AI and the attentional technologies is the pleasure and peculiarity in enjoying our own subjectivities.

5. If you knew a novel, or a poem or a screenplay was written using AI would it make any difference to how you responded to it as a reader or audience? Does the form of writing make any difference to your response—so, for example, if you knew a film you were watching had a script written using AI or, alternatively, if you were reading a novel written using AI? Does genre make any difference—for example, if you were reading a sonnet or an elegy, or if you were reading a science fiction short story, or if you were reading a video game script for an adventure game?

That there will be a part of humanity who refuse to engage with cultural products generated by AI. I'm on some author platforms and it's clear to me that some writers of Romance are and have been seeing their work as a series of 'guarantees' to the reader. They sell their writing as if it were white goods, with a guarantee of the 'friends to enemies' trope or the 'high value man' cliché. Some of the writers I've seen seem to very much know what their readers want and they spend considerable effort in providing an advertising pitch to let their readers know exactly what they are getting. This is a kind of approach to writing I can see as becoming reproducible by AI, because it often articulates itself as formula-led and AI is very good at iterations of clearly-defined formulae. This might not be a bad thing for writers of such Romance novels, as they might be able to produce the same kind of product with less effort and better proofing standards. Anyway, the authorial identities of such writers are often articulated more as a service-provider than an airy genius, so I can see this as an easy enough switch which readers may well not care about.

But for myself, if I could not tell if a work of literary fiction, a sonnet or something was generated by AI, then I'm not sure I'd have the epistemological basis to reject it out of hand. But I just used the term 'generated by AI' there, as if humans would not be involved in the process. But that's not the case. In order to ensure the match between intent and programming, human oversight would be an important element at many stages in the production of a literary product, as would human experimentation with AI to see the kinds of things it might produce that we currently have not quite experienced.

6. Does any AI have imagination? If so, in way or ways? It not, why not? Do you believe it could ever have imagination?

In the sense of AI having the capacity of some kind of internal subjective imaging, such as the way I might think of a pink elephant if you tell me not to think of a pink elephant, then no, I don't think so. I'll call this our 'internal imaging system' and come back to it in a bit.

Another way we understand imagination is the ability to make combinations of ideas, objects, materials, etc. into something which is novel, unusual or affecting in some new way. If this is what we mean by imagination, then I'd say yes, or at least believe that if AI does not currently have imagination, it will have. I know there might be the objection that an output based on a stochastic process which ends up being original (monkeys with typewriters eventually producing *Hamlet*) is the antithesis of imagination, but I don't think we are quite talking about this. Firstly, when we ask AI for something, it does not produce all the possible texts until it lands on *Hamlet* or *Fifty Shades of Grey* and we go (after a long, long time), 'Ah ha!'. AI today often gives us something quite usable after a request and a few follow-ups. Also, we can train the AI itself, for example by asking it to read *Macbeth* and Kyd's *The Spanish Tragedy* and then produce a play in the written style of the former with some of the same plot points as the latter, for example. I'm not saying we'll get *Hamlet*, but we will likely get something largely coherent and consistent.

So my answer is a qualified 'yes' to the question of if AI has imagination. But this brings me back to our internal imaging system, that which allows us to see a pink elephant, even though you just told me not to think about pink elephants (and do many other things). Because AI does not have, or perhaps need, an internal imaging system, we may yet find quite robust differences between how humans 'imagine' and how AI does it. We might be able to train ourselves to imagine in a certain way that

AI does not or is very costly to do and such differences might only come to light because of the ability of AI to imagine. This, however, is moving into the imaginaries of technology, and I think I'll leave the development of these thoughts for my next book.

7. The previous question touched on the notion of whether AI can itself be imaginative. The follow up, then, is whether it can (itself) form new ideas, have sensations, form memories? Can AI actually think? Can it feel?

Lord, I hate to be all philosophy 101 about it, but it really depends on what we mean by 'think' and 'feel'. But AI certainly encourages us to ask these questions, and to perhaps realise all along that different people might have been meaning different things by it.

I've avoided doing this so far, but I'd answer the question with a question, which I realise is a bad way to answer, most of the time. Here's my question: do we use the verbs 'think' and 'feel' when we are discussing AI? And if we do, are they useful for communicating with others? I think the answer to both these questions is a firm 'yes' and if not, we may find ourselves using 'think' and 'feel' more in future and again, using these terms in functional and useful ways when it comes to AI.

Now, I know philosophers tend to use words in different ways from plain Janes and standard Stevens. You wouldn't give rights to the fictional character Elizabeth Bennet because someone says, 'Elizabeth Bennet thinks deeply about other people's personalities'. And we don't think of calling welfare services if we say 'my wayfaring tree feels a bit abused since we let the rambling rose overtake the garden'. So I accept there's something we are getting at here about thinking and feeling, but I still think it's important to recognize that we apply those terms very often to AI and in ways which are perfectly serviceable.

And now I want to bring in our imaginaries of technology again, because at its imaginative limit, this question is about if we could ever afford the rights and privileges of humans to non-biological or non-human systems. If we think about science fiction, these questions abound, particularly in the *Star Trek* franchise with characters I grew up with like Commander Data (an android) and The Doctor (a hologram). And what I think these imaginative experiments tell us, is that if something can walk like a duck and quack like a duck then we'll probably treat it like a duck. And if it can demand the vote, be an honorable and consistent friend and tell you in convincing terms which Shakespeare play is its favorite, then we'll probably start treating it like a human. In all this, I think it will depend less on the internal process going on inside 'the machine' and more about the behaviors we experience. I mean, how else did we work out that other humans were humans, other than behavior?

So, I don't know yet if AI can think and feel, but I'm certainly open to the possibility, even if this means perhaps shifting slightly what we mean by 'think' and 'feel'.

8. It might have been impossible for someone from the medieval period, where the quill was the primary writing tool and parchment the medium, to imagine a world in which word processors existed. Speculating as much as you like, what do you imagine the writing world will look like in 20 years, 50 years, 200 years?

I like the historical analogy here, because one of the principal ways we develop technological imaginaries is through comparison with the past.

Take the history of the visual arts, particularly the emergence of commercially-viable photography in the 19th Century. Photography was seen, quite rightly, as a threat to painting because it could do what painting did in a fraction of time and with greater consistency and, arguable, fidelity. Of course I used the term 'what painting did' in a slightly provocative way, because anyone familiar with modern fine art painting will know that it is very much alive and painters still make a living from painting. The natural question is then: What did painting do in the face of photography? And the think the answer is (a) abstraction and (b) a focus on the physical qualities of paint itself. And as an aside, I think b leant itself very well to a. To put it another way, painting went where photography was not or could not go.

The question about the future of creative writing could be put this way: Where can human writing go where AI writing is not or could not? I'm not suggesting I know the answer to that question, but what I'm fairly confident in is that we will adapt and push different kinds of literature and written experiences because of AI.

Though in this process, I do think that much human-made creative writing will cease or be significantly curtailed. And the closer that writing is to formula, the easier it will be to get AI to do the job. And you know, it is likely to do a more consistent and efficient job of it than us humans. I think writers need to be prepared for that and to see AI as a tool to use, as well as experimenting with what non-AI writing might be and look like.

In the narrative arts, a response to AI may lead to a new way of looking at live performance by humans. This might not be the writing-per-se, but liveness and literature, I think, will likely come to be valued differently in a cultural landscape where AI produces a significant amount of cultural output. We may see a resurgence in theatre, in storytelling, or the emergence of quite new forms of artistic interaction, where a group of people make up a story communally in order to find out more about one another or about a certain event or subject: A kind of live non-digital creative commons.

But there's another thing to note, if we go back to the painting/photography analogy again. While fine art painting responded to photography in certain ways, it also of course used photography, so much so that if today we saw a photograph on canvas amid some painted surfaces, we would not consider it radical form-subversion, but simply 'mixed-media'. Artforms doing only develop reactively as a response to the emergence other artforms, they also merge and negotiate with other art forms, so that music, literature, fine art and games might all be manifest in a single work.

All I'm confident of is that writers will experiment within and without AI. AI will become a dynamic tool for writers in ways we can already see, such as proofreading, offering 'in the style of' examples we might copy or emulate, or in providing summary and analysis of texts we have produced. And in a qualified and probably undramatic way, it will do some of the things our imaginaries suggest, partly because we were creative enough to come up with those imaginaries.

9. If you had all the time you needed, what written work would you like to write and why? It doesn't have to be a work of creative writing. Would you use AI to write it; and, if so, how would you use it?

For years, I've spent time reading, watching and listening to material about AI without really using it and it's only in the last 6 months or so that I've been exploring chatbots and being very impresses with the results. I know now that my use of the technology is only going to increase, partly to make my life easier but also because I'm interested, as I said at the start, in the ways tech shapes our lives and intellectual history too.

But to answer the question, I'd like to write a short novel called *TagTeam* about a brother and a sister who get involved in pro-wrestling after their mother dies. All the best stories begin with dead mothers. The book would be written in a tag team structure, with AI writing one chapter and then me writing another. I'd ask the AI for rewrites of their chapters as I saw fit and I'd ask for suggestions from the AI about my chapters, but there would a fairly strict separation of labor. The formal overlap between the content of the work, its structure and its method would be a good way, I hope, of exploring some of these writer/AI interactions.

And even with this outline, it's clear to me that we are well into the age of AI creative writing and that writers, me among them, are interested to play. And playing is key, because that's how we might be able to better see and express the meanings of a new age, and perhaps the meaning of some past ones too.

10. Who benefits most from using AI? Anyone more than anyone else? Any industry more than any other industry? Any place or places in the world? Do you think more people or fewer people might write creatively because of the existence and application of AI—if so, why; if not, why not?

This brings me right back to our imaginaries of technology, whose dystopian tendencies tend to suggest a situation in which our democratic sensibilities and egalitarian aspirations are frustrated by tech. We see this in our concerns about genetic science in the form of eugenics, where gene therapy which makes 'superior' humans of those who can pay. We can see it in concerns around the tech/human interface, and the rise of the cyborg which will lead to robotically enhanced humans, again, for those who can pay. We saw it with cryogenic technology in the 1990s, where the super-rich attempted to extend their lives by being frozen until science has found a cure for the thing they died of. The promise was immortality, though I think we are only one power cut away from that project failing.

So if our imaginaries are anything to go by, then it's the already rich and powerful who stand to benefit most from AI, whether they actually use it or not. Though one aspect of this is also about those who benefit *least* from AI. And the answer to this seems clear enough to be: Those who cannot use AI or whose use of it is limited. And who might these people be? Well, presumably anyone without access to the internet, anyone who is illiterate, speaks a language that does not possess a correspondingly rich large language model (LLM) or anyone not educated to use AI. The risk of any technology from the perspective of anyone with democratic and egalitarian sensibilities is that it can exacerbate inequality, making lives easier and more productive for the privileged and the inverse for those not-so-privileged. That's the worst-case scenario of our imaginaries.

But we need other imaginaries too, because the future is an uncertain place. So let's think about the audio revolution I lived through during the years, roughly, between 2001–2008. When I was an Undergraduate, I was in bands and did some sound engineering jobs to pay for time in a local recording studio. The studio itself was filled with outboard equipment that each controlled individual effects such as reverb, chorus, EQ and other things. It required lots of time, lots of money and lots of expertise to even be a mediocre sound engineer. But in the years after this, I saw the end of the studio, or at least if not the end, then the significant broadening out of who could record, mix and master music to a high quality. New audio editing software and great UX design made audio editing intuitive, quick and powerful. One example I'd mention is software Audacity, which is free and has some amazing capabilities and I had a friend whose band signed to a major label on the basis of a home recorded and mixed album. Against our more apocalyptic imaginaries then, the audio editing revolution has made it more likely that those without cash or connecting can enter in a meaningful way into the musical world and for anyone with democratic and egalitarian sensibilities, this seems like a good thing.

But, I hear you say, what will happen to writers when publishing houses have AI-generated smash-hit whodunits? What will happen to writing when AI can dish out better haiku than Basho? Apart from some publishing houses and their shareholders, won't many lose out both economically and creatively?

The answer is maybe, and it will depend very much on how government regulates the sector and invests in the skills of their citizens. Though it seems to me that AI will offer the opportunity for many people without certain skills to write, for example people with specific learning disabilities, like dyslexia (I'm a dyslexic who writes, but I know it can be a real challenge for some to get their ideas down on the page). And AI, it seems to me, will not foreclose on our ability to write for ourselves, nor the goods of doing so. My optimistic imaginaries about AI take me to a place where creative writing is easier and quicker in some ways due to AI, but also crucially it would be a field full of experimentation, with and without AI. There are new forms and values of creative writing we have not yet conceived of. There are wheels out there not to be reinvented, but to be discovered.

Nikunj Jain

Abstract **Nikunj Jain** says: artificial intelligence intersects with creativity, language, and the future of storytelling. Coding backend systems and observing AI's task efficiency it is possible to quickly identify AI as a powerful tool for aiding articulation and for overcoming writer's block. It is, nevertheless, not an autonomous creative force and, likewise, it is capable of understanding emotion or timing or exhibiting empathy. Rather, it can be a 'thought stater', a generator of playful reinterpretations of classic stories, enabling interactive, personalized narratives. The danger might be in creating derivative stories, a danger that future heightens the significance of human prompts. That said, it is with AI that there is the possibility of creating multisensory, time-dissolving books, powered by brainwave interfaces. Here science fiction meets current science, possibility builds from the interaction of human and machine. While true imagination and feelings is unlikely possible in AI, it does have the capacity to democratize creative expression, especially for non-native speakers and children. Perhaps, though, the core question is not who writes but who has the time to read in a world of infinite output. In that context, compression and curation might become as important as creativity.

Keywords Imagination · Prompt · Multisensory · Articulation · Compression

G. Harper (ed.), *AI and Creative Writing*,
https://doi.org/10.1007/978-3-031-99101-1_9

Nikunj Jain Is a creative thinker who has dedicated his career to fostering innovation across various industries. With a diverse background encompassing Mechanical Engineering from Virginia Tech, Transportation Styling from the College for Creative Studies in Detroit, and an MBA in Marketing Strategy from the SPJ Institute of Management & Research in India, Nikunj brings a unique perspective to problem-solving.

His approach involves viewing challenges from multiple angles—Strategy, Technology, Design, and Creative Business Models. Nikunj believes in the power of chaos to challenge conventional thinking and drive innovation. He has written extensively on topics such as imagination, creativity, preparing for challenge innovation, and cultivating an innovative organizational culture.

Through his work and writings, Nikunj aims to inspire others to embrace unconventional thinking and drive positive change.

1. When someone says 'Artificial Intelligence' what things do you think about?

A human coding an algorithm—I have seen the backend of a leading Indian IT company that supports chat AI for major automotive brands; it was a list of questions the brand would give and the IT company would create links of what should be answered if that question came up. To summarize, it was Reducing repetitive tasks to be handled by a machine that learns the task and applies its back-end list to keep the task moving.

2. Thinking of antonyms of 'intelligence', would it be possible, do you think, to have 'Artificial Unintelligence' or 'Artificial Stupidity' or 'Artificial Awkwardness' and, if so, what might they look like?

Intelligence is multifaceted—thought the common idea is related to Knowledge, Calculability and Application, there are other elements such as emotional intelligence. Something that Artificial Awkwardness would not be able to resolve, the right time to share bad/good information.

Emotion is what makes us human & intelligent. We are often frustrated with Siri/Alexa/ChatGPT when you ask a question, and the answer doesn't suit your need—your personal state of emotion determines what answer you expect. Hence the term 'walking on eggshells'.

3. What kinds of things can AI help creative writers do? What kind of AI might help them best?

Creative writing comes down to the plot whether it's the main character being killed off or a sudden revival of old. We often talk about writer's block; AI would help become the thought starter for some of these blocks. A fun application would be taking the same book and writing it in multiple different ways; we write the seven dwarfs if it was written by Snoop Dogg, or rewrite the satirical fable by George Orwell, *Animal Farm* as thought it was a rap battle. A kindle book that evolves the story in real time based on your favorite character.

4. What things can AI not help creative writers do? (and this could be specifically associated with their writing or more generally in their lives)

The start—if there is no prompt there is no story. For creative writers the base line story is critical, that's where the limits of AI stop.

Personally, I see AI as the threat to creative writers, a parallel to the infinite monkey theorem. Will new content ever be created or just the same old ones with a slight plot twist to keep sales going?

5. If you knew a novel, or a poem or a screenplay was written using AI would it make any difference to how you responded to it as a reader or audience? Does the form of writing make any difference to your response—so, for example, if you knew a film you were watching had a script written using AI or, alternatively, if you were reading a novel written using AI? Does genre make any difference—for example, if you were reading a sonnet or an elegy, or if you were reading a science fiction short story, or if you were reading a video game script for an adventure game?

I see this in two ways:

1. Roko's basilisk—Do I still watch knowing that if tomorrow there is an uprising, and I had supportive ideologies for Super AI or should I not watch the movie/read the book—hinting that I don't support the SuperAI takeover.
2. I come home from a busy day teaching at OU and have 30 minutes to watch a mild action movie with enough of a plot twist that my

tired brain can keep up. It's simply entertainment for my limited time on a preferred Genre, nothing more, who's to say the latest *House of Dragon* (Condal and Martin) is not written in some form by ChatGPT?

6. Does any AI have imagination? If so, in way or ways? It not, why not? Do you believe it could ever have imagination?

Short answer—I don't believe AI has Imagination.

AI's imagination is a factor of the coders imagination and the prompt command given. If the Machine Learning—Data Analyst had a creative mind to say generate a random hex code color and apply it to any animal, the output would be a blue colored giraffe. However, our imagination is a factor of life experiences and ability to connect random dots to make humor or a scary movie, if we code that into an algorithm then yes, I am capturing my way of imagination into the AI.

7. The previous question touched on the notion of whether AI can itself be imaginative. The follow up, then, is whether it can (itself) form new ideas, have sensations, form memories? Can AI actually think? Can it feel?

Oooo the f word... feelings. That's scary, being rude to your Alexa only to find out your next Amazon delivery got sent to the wrong address mysteriously. Today there are already cameras picking facial gestures to study emotion, an easy plug for AI to pick up and integrate. I don't believe there will be any reason for AI to have feelings but rather reciprocate the emotional state we are in.

8. It might have been impossible for someone from the medieval period, where the quill was the primary writing tool and parchment the medium, to imagine a world in which word processors existed. Speculating as much as you like, what do you imagine the writing world will look like in 20 years, 50 years, 200 years?

In the distant future, the concept of writing itself might evolve beyond our current understanding. Technologies such as quantum computing and advanced AI, the very act of creating stories could become a fully immersive, collective, and instantaneous process.

I imagine the Babel fish from the book *The Hitchhikers Guide to the Galaxy* (Adams), feeding or our own brainwaves to power an AI Copilot (Neuralink)—a multisensory experience to writing. We have experience books that have scratch pads to evoke smell, imagine writing that is shape shifting based on the temperature of the book. Or a book that doesn't observe time, every day it evolves or dissolves.

9. If you had all the time you needed, what written work would you like to write and why? It doesn't have to be a work of creative writing. Would you use AI to write it; and, if so, how would you use it?

Time itself is an interesting thing to capture. One of my favorite movies is *Arrival* (Villeneuve), an alien movie unlike the traditional genre of alien movies. The premise lies in communicating without time, no past-present-future. Imagine Shakespeare writing *Romeo and Juliet* (Shakespeare) next to you based on your life. I see application of AI to write multisensory pieces; capturing the experience of eating fresh cut jackfruit in the dense forest of India.

10. Who benefits most from using AI? Anyone more than anyone else? Any industry more than any other industry? Any place or places in the world? Do you think more people or fewer people might write creatively because of the existence and application of AI—if so, why; if not, why not?

I do believe AI helps writers who are creative but not articulative. I believe I fall in that category, and so does my 8-year-old nephew who wrote a book about a hiker lost in the Andes. Create the storyline, the plot twists and then let the AI run with it to articulate the imagination into words.

Words, after all, for non-English speakers, that is the key. I understand the dire effect of Plagiarism, however every company today is fighting its employees from using ChatGPT to help craft better emails or write a more professional sounding executive summary. It is only a matter of time that we open the flood gates and everyone is an author.

The problem is not the writing, it's the reverse—who has the time to read it?—the following is the solution:

ChatGPT—please compress this entire document down to one paragraph'—**Output:** The text discusses various aspects and implications of AI in creative writing. It explores the concept of AI being used to reduce repetitive tasks and aid in writing by providing prompts and creative inspiration. The text also speculates on the potential for AI to create 'Artificial Unintelligence' or 'Artificial Stupidity' and considers the emotional intelligence aspect that AI lacks. It debates the role of AI in helping writers overcome blocks, generate diverse versions of stories, and evolve narratives in real-time. The limitations of AI in generating original story prompts are highlighted, as well as concerns about AI's impact on creativity and originality. The potential for AI to have imagination and emotions is discussed, concluding that while AI can simulate aspects of creativity, it lacks true human-like imagination and feelings. The text also speculates on the future of writing, envisioning immersive, multisensory experiences and evolving narratives. Finally, it considers the benefits of AI for non-native English speakers and creative individuals who struggle with articulation, suggesting that AI could democratize authorship but also raises concerns about who will have the time to read the abundance of AI-generated content.

References

Adams, Douglas. 1980. *The Hitchhiker's Guide to the Galaxy*. New York: Harmony Books.

Condal, Ryan, and George R. R. Martin (creators). 2022. *House of the Dragon*. HBO Entertainment and Warner Bros.

Orwell, George. 2021. *Animal Farm*. London: Collins Classics.

Shakespeare, William. 2000. *Romeo and Juliet*, 1597. Oxford: Published for the Malone Society by Oxford University Press.

Villeneuve, Denis. 2016. *Arrival*. Paramount Pictures.

Josie Barnard

Abstract **Josie Barnard** says: AI reshapes the conditions of writing, authorship, and meaning-making. AI is not solely a technological innovation it also produces sociocultural consequences, especially in creative domains. AI systems, trained on vast datasets, reinforce dominant linguistic patterns and values, leading to the homogenization of language and thought. Writing produced with AI tools often substitutes surface-level fluency for depth, erasing ambiguity, contradiction, and the richness of human subjectivity. AI encourages forms of aestheticization and narrative resolution that flatten complexity and marginalize voices that resist easy classification. This can involve the reduction of language to metadata—treating meaning as extractable and quantifiable—and thereby stripping writing of its political, emotional, and lived dimensions. Being vigilant about resisting this, we must adopt a conscious practice of creative writing that refuses automation when it compromises imagination, risk, or cultural specificity. Ultimately, writers and readers alike need to protect the open-ended, uncertain, and affective qualities that make literature a site of struggle, transformation, and plural meaning.

Keywords Metadata · Aestheticization · Erasure · Homogenization · Cultural

G. Harper (ed.), *AI and Creative Writing*,
https://doi.org/10.1007/978-3-031-99101-1_10

Dr. Josie Barnard SFHEA is Associate Professor of Creative and Digital Practice at De Montfort University, where she is School Lead for Digital Pedagogies. She is the award-winning author of six books, extensive print and broadcast journalism and international academic articles and chapters. Her digital inclusion research, which is the subject of a Research Excellence Framework REF2021 Impact Case Study (*Bridging the Digital Divide: Creativity research resulting in digital upskilling*), is represented by her monograph *The Multimodal Writer: Creative Writing Across Genres and Media* (Bloomsbury, 2019) and her BBC Radio 4 program, *Digital Future: the New Underclass* (2019). She is, alongside writers including Dame Penelope Lively and Sir Roy Strong, the subject of a chapter in Sue Gee's *Just You and the Page: Twelve writers and their art* (Seren, 2021). Josie is invited co-editor of a Special Issue of the international academic journal *Writing in Practice* (2022) on the subject of her multimodal writing research. Her new digital for creativity research is represented by outputs including 'Cyber Nuts and Bolts' for *Convergence: The International Journal of Research into New Media Technologies* (2023) and 'Creating creativity for future-proofing digital engagement, an evidence-based approach' in Palgrave's *Digital Inclusion: International Policy and Research* (2024). She collaborates with government departments and other key stakeholder groups to inform policy and develop digital inclusion.

1. When someone says 'Artificial Intelligence' what things do you think about?

'Artificial Intelligence' makes me think of the power of metaphor.

The term 'Artificial Intelligence' was famously coined in 1955. Picture the scene: a young Assistant Professor of Mathematics, John McCarthy, wanted to stage a summer school at Dartmouth in the US to discuss an emerging field of research. He needed funding, so he needed the project to sound exciting. In his funding application, McCarthy chose to use the term 'Artificial Intelligence'. It was just a term, but it stuck. It captured people's imagination.

Artificial Intelligence (AI) is often anthropomorphised. When Artificial Intelligence (AI) produces false results, it is said to be 'hallucinating' or 'lying'. Random prediction on the basis of insufficient data might be a better way of describing what happens when AI produces this kind of result.

Metaphor is used to promote and generate exciting hype about AI, and to explain its limitations. 'Stochastic parrots' is a term indicating that even if AI generates convincing language, that's not because AI 'thinks', rather, it 'parrots' (Bender et al. 2021). Sticking with the natural world for imagery, Bender and Koller's (2020) 'Octopus Paper' uses an imagined octopus to explain some of the practicalities of how AI works: two people, A and B, are stranded on separate islands; they find they can communicate via telegraph; an especially smart octopus in the sea works out how to tap into their telegraph; soon, affected by loneliness, the octopus cuts B out and, on basis of A and B's prior chats, pretends to be B, and is believed; however, when a bear attacks A and A asks for help, the octopus—submerged and removed—has no referents, it has no idea how A can fashion protection from an angry bear, because the bear is new to the octopus, aka AI. Thus the piece uses a wily octopus and an angry bear to explain how AI is limited to 'scraping' pre-existing data. Metaphors can help us understand new concepts.

However, metaphors can also slip into common parlance, we can easily 'forget that they are indeed just metaphors; they can be misleading, and they can also work as self-fulfilling prophecies because they fully occupy an unfamiliar phenomenon even after it becomes less so' (Ganesh 2022: 60). One way to mitigate such misunderstanding may be to describe what AI does in a more prosaic way. Alternative terms that have been suggested include 'Automated Pattern Recognition' (Hunger 2023) and, 'Systematic Approaches to Learning Algorithms and Machine Inferences', with this last becoming, for short, 'SALAMI' (Quinta 2019). 'Now we have redefined the name … Will SALAMI have emotions? Can SALAMI acquire a 'personality' similar to humans' ?' (ibid.). Call 'Artificial Intelligence' something different and it could perhaps be more easily conceptualized as a tool.

Some of the hype around AI is that it will replace humans. Certainly, jobs are already being lost to AI. And AI's 'scraping' is fast becoming more sophisticated (George 2024). As cognitive scientist Margaret Boden frames it, computers can '*appear*' to be creative (2004)—and, that capacity will continue to improve. However, Boden also flags that what goes on in the human mind in terms of the interplay of motivation and emotion when creative ideas are forming is highly complex, rich, subtle and, above all, idiosynchratic (Boden 2004: 322). AI doesn't operate in a vacuum. There are many 'intriguing relations between creativity and computers' (Boden 2004: 10). A 'relational rather than ontological approach to computational creativity and, more broadly, AI' places 'humans at the centre of analysis' (Natale and Henrickson 2024: 1920).

When I think of AI and its potential for creativity as 'relational'—with humans very firmly factored in—then the potential for creative writers to collaborate with AI can become exciting.

2. Thinking of antonyms of 'intelligence', would it be possible, do you think, to have 'Artificial Unintelligence' or 'Artificial Stupidity' or 'Artificial Awkwardness' and, if so, what might they look like?

Examples of 'Artificial Awkwardness' are the AI-generated hands that have too many fingers. 'If [AI] can't understand the 3D nature of a hand or the context of a situation, it will struggle to accurately recreate it' (Bentley in Hughes 2023). AI-generated beer adverts that went viral for showing people who swerve glasses and cans of beer 'demonically' away from their mouths (Zilber 2023), too, can be described as 'Artificial Awkwardness' (AA). When 'ChatGPT' produces a false claim, rather than describing it as 'hallucinating', it's been proposed that we should talk of ChatGPT 'bullshitting' (Hicks et al. 2024). Hence, 'Artificial Bullshitting' (AB) can be added to the list.

3. What kinds of things can AI help creative writers do? What kind of AI might help them best?

I'll start with two words: writer's block. As novelist Amos Oz puts it, 'A blank page is actually a whitewashed wall with no door and no window. Beginning to tell a story is like making a pass at a total stranger'. (1999: 2).

I've written six books, over 50 radio features and over a dozen radio programmes, and I've lost count of the number of articles that I've written. But it doesn't mean I find the blank page easy to negotiate. And I haven't spoken to a single writer who does.

If those first thoughts are slow in coming, AI may be helpful in terms of getting words flowing. For this task, generative AI is a collaborator. Typing a few words and prompts to generate a bit of AI text could serve as a useful starting point. The blank page can be off-putting because it somehow links straight through to the end product (will the finished novel/film/TV series sell, what will people think?). The act of assembling words and prompts for AI may help writers become immersed in enjoyment of the *process* of creation (Harper 2015). Webb and Brien suggest that during the creative process creative writers are a cross between a bowerbird, which seeks out all the blue things with which to make its nest, and a '*bricoleur*', or, jack of all trades, who makes do with what's available (2012: 198–201). The act of assembling apparently random words and prompts to see what generative AI makes of them would almost invariably reveal a pattern and so could contribute to the creative process.

Another way generative AI can be used is to stimulate criticality. One exercise I do with my Creative Writing undergraduate students involves the fairytale *Three Billy Goats Gruff* and an AI-generated precis. Repetition is often targeted if an editor is looking to make cuts. But repetition is often key for fairytales. It can help build tension. Thus, in the uncut, repetition-rich fairytale (Ashliman 2000), first the youngest goat crosses the bridge, persuading the troll to wait for the next goat which, in turn, persuades the troll to wait for the largest goat of all. Cuts and changes made by one AI tool to effect a precis included losing two of the billy goats and ending bathetically with a single goat crossing the bridge with a 'grumble' and no troll in sight. The AI precis tool colour-coded all the changes, so it was Sossible to systematically go through the precis and apply criticality to each change in turn. Here, then, AI is an example of how *not* to do it. The tension-free AI precis served as a great provocation and the basis of a pedagogical session on editing and close-reading.

The business of being a creative writer—that is, the practical side of making a living while writing (Lahire 2010)—is likely to benefit from AI. Practical tasks such as writing funding applications or letters to literary agents, for example, could be expedited. The results would have to be personalized, naturally, but first drafts could be generated by AI.

And of course, the business of AI is providing a rich set of circumstances and characters that can be turned into fiction—of which, more later.

4. What things can AI not help creative writers do? (and this could be specifically associated with their writing or more generally in their lives)

It may seem that generative AI can help creative writers cheat.

The launch in 2022 of ChatGPT immediately triggered worries that students would use ChatGPT to write their papers. Almost as quickly, new methods of detecting ChatGPT-generated content were developed, and high levels of accuracy have already been achieved (Oghaz et al. 2023). Will AI or the detectors win? In the context of creative writing, that's not the key point. It's the experience of working to pull the text into shape that writers generally enjoy. As Cynthia Ozick notes, 'a redemptive literature, a literature that interprets and decodes the world, beaten out for the sake of humanity, must wrestle with its own body, with its own flesh and blood, with its own life' (1996: 136). It's part of the job, it's part of the fun: writers 'wrestle' with words. AI can provide, as Clarke puts it 'creativity amplification' whereby AI chatbots, for example, may become 'extensions of and partners in the writer's creativity' (2022: 141). But it's the writers who inject the play and strategic experimentation; writers bring the creativity.

AI can support and contribute. It can add stimulation and possibilities; it can be a tool and a chatty work mate. It cannot give the heady, messy experience of wrestling to produce the writing. That experience belongs to the creative writer.

5. If you knew a novel, or a poem or a screenplay was written using AI would it make any difference to how you responded to it as a reader or audience? Does the form of writing make any difference to your response—so, for example, if you knew a film you were watching had a script written using AI or, alternatively, if you were reading a novel written using AI? Does genre make any difference—for example, if you were reading a sonnet or an elegy, or if you were reading a science fiction short story, or if you were reading a video game script for an adventure game?

If someone says of a creative work, 'It reads/sounds as if it was written by AI', it's not generally meant as praise. Such comments suggest that the work is clichéd and/or formulaic.

ChatGPT launched in 2022. In 2023, Amazon put a cap on the number of AI-generated books any individual author can publish on Amazon—although, the limit was set at what many judged to be a pretty high three books per author per *day* (Creamer 2023). Readers value human creativity. Well-established literary traditions centre on readers getting to know something of the person who wrote the book. Those traditions include the author interview (whereby authors tell newspaper or broadcast interviewers secrets of their writing process) and the author tour (whereby an author reads their book to a live audience and signs copies in person). Far from dying out in face of the fourth industrial revolution, literary festivals experienced exponential growth (Barnard 2019: 19). The authors' 'real presence'—their mingling and chat—gives readers, notes Meehan (2005), the 'impression of a special kind of intertextual and even inter-authorial buzz, as [readers] move steadily through the narrative of the festival'. 'In an era in which remote digital communications can make us feel alienated and isolated, live interactions are perhaps more important than ever for authors' (Barnard 2019: 19).

That said, when the rapper Drake joined parody rapper Snowd4y on stage for a remix of his 'Hey There Delilah' cover, 'Wah Gwan Delilah', his appearance did not clear up the question of whether the lyrics had been generated by AI or Drake; Drake posted the song to his Instagram story, and this was taken by some as confirmation of authorship (Watercutter 2024). Articles suggest that 'the track's ridiculous lyrics and the off-kilter audio quality of Drake's vocals' (Robinson 2024) prove that AI was involved. As this chapter goes to press, neither Drake nor Snowd4y have confirmed or denied the AI rumours. The cult of personality can make a work appealing, and so can an air of AI-fuelled mystery.

6. Does any AI have imagination? If so, in way or ways? It not, why not? Do you believe it could ever have imagination?

AI can, to adopt Boden's framing (2004), *appear* to have imagination. As noted, AI scrapes data from the World Wide Web. That data is finite and will at some point run out, possibly quite soon if the current pace of data-scraping continues (Villalobos et al. 2024). There are numerous examples of AI-generated stories that are either absurdly garbled or dully formulaic and lacking spark. AI companies' efforts to change that include employing journalists, published novelists and academics to provide AI training (George 2024). These selected writers are reportedly paid well for providing AI models with 'gold standard' material designed to 'improve the quality of chatbot replies' and reduce the chances of AI errors (ibid.). AI's version of imagination is likely to look increasingly convincing, certainly.

Returning to McCarthy's 1955 Dartmouth proposal, the original document has a comment on the links between 'AI' and creativity. Under the heading 'Randomness and Creativity', the document says: 'A fairly attractive and yet clearly incomplete conjecture is that the difference between creative thinking and unimaginative competent thinking lies in the injection of a some [sic] randomness. The randomness must be guided by intuition to be efficient. In other words, the educated guess or the hunch include controlled randomness in otherwise orderly thinking'. (McCarthy et al. 1955). AI can't do 'intuition', it can't have a 'hunch'. However, an imaginative trainer may inject 'controlled randomness' (Dowsett et al. 2023). Algorithms search out typical; on the edges of the typical results, there may be some atypical data that could be targeted as part of the training and added into the mix with 'controlled randomness' that appears to be imaginative and/or may help trigger imaginative solutions in human users. A bit of such controlled AI randomness could be helpful for creative writers if, for example, they've got past the writer's block but have arrived at a structural problem and need a few potential solutions to weigh up, play with and refashion.

7. The previous question touched on the notion of whether AI can itself be imaginative. The follow up, then, is whether it can (itself) form new ideas, have sensations, form memories? Can AI actually think? Can it feel?

Some robots already have a version of physical sensations via electrical impulses (Paridon 2023). Robots used in surgery need to have sensitive hands that can effect nuanced movements, so it seems likely that such robots will quickly become more sophisticated. Memories are arguably already in place for AI, if information scraped from the web is framed as memories. Just as AI can appear to have imagination, AI can appear to 'think'.

In his famous 1950 paper 'Computing Machinery and Intelligence', Alan Turing asks 'Can machines think?', and says the question is 'too meaningless to deserve discussion' (1950: 442). However, Turing then says, 'Nevertheless I believe that at the end of the century the use of words and general educated opinion will have altered so much that one will be able to speak of machines thinking without expecting to be contradicted' (ibid.: 442). As Turing foresaw, the idea that machines can think is now widely accepted.

In the context of creative writing, 'thinking' AI can be a useful literary device. Of the many explorations, one is Kazuo Ishiguro's *Klara and the Sun* (2021), a novel that uses a robot narrator—Klara, an 'Artificial Friend'—to explore what it is to love. Ishiguro's book is not, it seems to me, an exploration of *whether* robots can love. Rather, the novel uses an imagined robot which has the advantage, in terms of storytelling craft, of a lack of knowledge. This lack of knowledge enables the robot's experience to serve as a prism that provides a fresh perspective on an age-old human problem. Regardless of whether or not AI can actually think, the notion remains a useful literary device.

8. It might have been impossible for someone from the medieval period, where the quill was the primary writing tool and parchment the medium, to imagine a world in which word processors existed. Speculating as much as you like, what do you imagine the writing world will look like in 20 years, 50 years, 200 years?

What will the writing world look like in years to come? I address this issue with my book *The Multimodal Writer* (2019): how can writers stay resilient in a writing and publishing landscape that is characterised by fast-paced change (Barnard 2019: 6); how can they 'future-proof' their writing practice? The Internet and Web 2.0 technology proved transformative (ibid.: 16); COVID lockdowns forced different relationships with our increasingly online world (Barnard 2023); generative AI has brought new, seismic shifts. 'Future-proofing' isn't just about protection—it's about making the most of amazing opportunities. We each have different skills, experiences and aims. *The Multimodal Writer* provides theory and practice—including a model of creativity that can be personalized (Barnard 2019: 85–89; 2024)—to help each individual writer optimally leverage their own internal resources to address challenges and make the most of opportunities in the digital sphere as they arise. A key resource for each of us is what I term 'remediation of practice', whereby 'as new challenges and opportunities arise, a writer who remediates his or her own practice 'looks to existing skills and prior experience and adapts or applies them in new contexts as part of a process of, in effect, collaborating with him or herself'. (Barnard 2019: 29). Another key resource is affect (Barnard 2023), including the sheer heft associated with 'vintage' technologies. AI is out there in the ether. By contrast, a particular fountain pen (it's weight in the hand and drag on the paper) can *feel* good to use.

One of my academic research projects, 'Digital Creativity Live at the Museum', involves using vintage technologies in fun activities designed to develop not just digital skills but, rather, computational knowledge that empowers. Partners for the project include Professor of Computing Christine Goutrié in Berlin and, in the UK, Leicester Museums and Galleries (LM&G). We've been using vintage telephones and typewriters to enable participants' development of (respectively) knowledge of binary code and algorithms (for discussion see DMU, 2022a; b). LM&G typewriters used in the activities include an 'up strike' 1874 Sholes and Glidden, a 'down strike' 1897 Blickendsderfer 7 and a 'front strike' 1940 Imperial Model T. The typewriters played a practical part in helping participants gain knowledge of how algorithms work (the problem of learning how to use a typewriter involves following a set of rules; an algorithm is a process or set of rules to be followed in problem-solving operations). And, the typewriters remind that all technology was new once. Some participants remembered using typewriters themselves, and this was reassuring (if a typewriter can be learned, so can a new function on a smartphone). Other, younger participants had only seen typewriters in films, yet still found the typewriters to be a reassuring reminder that all technology was new once. They felt empowered by the connections they could see, such as the QWERTY keyboard, which was invented in the nineteenth century and has survived moves from manual typewriters to electric typewriters to desktop computers to smartphones.

So, what does the future look like for writers? In terms of writing tools, I think the QWERTY keyboard will stay in use, so too the pencil. Writing tends to be a physical activity; the thinking process is often knitted in with the actions of forming letters with a pen or pencil on a page and/or striking out a sentence on a QWERTY keyboard (and then using the delete button or cut-and-paste tool) and/or procrastinating by making a coffee and/or scrumpling up a piece of paper and throwing it in the bin (Barnard 2019: 43–69).

Yet, some of the most important parts of the writing process (the protracted ruminations; the flashes of inspiration) often happen at unexpected or downright inconvenient moments, such as whilst in the shower or on a run. For this, in my imagination, the future provides a free-floating bot which hovers ethereally nearby and, via electrical impulses, captures those thoughts for later. Thank you, bot.

9. If you had all the time you needed, what written work would you like to write and why? It doesn't have to be a work of creative writing. Would you use AI to write it; and, if so, how would you use it?

AI issues that currently preoccupy me centre on damage that's being done. If I had all the time I needed to write, I would address these issues in a novel. I'd take inspiration from works such as Charles Dickens' *Oliver Twist* (1838) and Pat Barker's *Regeneration* (1991) which, respectively, interrogate through fiction the toll taken on humans of the nineteenth century English Poor Laws and the mental health of soldiers returning from the First World War.

AI is trained by humans, but those humans often suffer low wages and often terrible psychological consequences since 'training' may involve 'data cleaning' that includes filtering out inappropriate, stressful content (see, for example: Crawford 2021; Williams, 2024; Graham and Cant 2024). The scale of the toll on the natural world of the training process is becoming clear (see e.g. Bender et al. 2021); AI models like ChatGPT are 'thirsty', consuming vast quantities of water—'global AI demand may even require 4.2 – 6.6 billion cubic meters of water withdrawal in 2027, which is more than the total annual water withdrawal of … half of the United Kingdom' (Ren 2023). AI discriminates (see e.g. Noble's *Algorithms of Oppression*, 2018). AI is often anthropomorphized in ways that are problematically gendered (see e.g. Strengers and Kennedy 2020; Fournier-Tombs 2023). The AI hype can be highly convincing (for discussion, see the DAIR *Mystery AI Hype Theatre 3000* podcast, for example, DAIR 2022) and feel overwhelming. A pivot 'away from the machines and their risk of biases, and towards humans and the risks to their rights' (Prabhakaran et al. 2022) is needed. This fiction would be such a pivot.

Why do this? Dickens and Barker make complex, potentially 'dry' issues live and breathe. AI is developing so fast and in so many directions with so many implications all at once that it can be hard to feel we have got, or could ever get a handle on it. Fiction can be that handle. Fiction can capture the truth of complex issues.

Would I use AI to write it? No. But, I would consider using AI to generate text for a linked social media strand. This strand would give two or three of the novel's characters their own social media accounts and invite audience discussion of which elements were AI-generated. An aim here would be to contribute to learning regarding the differences between storylines that have been written by humans and those that are generated by AI.

10. Who benefits most from using AI? Anyone more than anyone else? Any industry more than any other industry? Any place or places in the world? Do you think more people or fewer people might write creatively because of the existence and application of AI—if so, why; if not, why not?

Tech corporations benefit most from AI. Publishers—of books, films, TV series—may benefit in the short term. Book publishers are already quite extensively using AI-generated illustrations and translations, for example. A 2024 Society of Authors survey found that 'A quarter of illustrators (26%) and over a third of translators (36%) have already lost work due to generative AI' (SOA 2024). However, as indicated, a number of gremlins are still working their way through the business of AI.

For one thing, AI-generated texts and scripts include errors, sometimes dangerous errors. Incidents to hit the headlines include: a supermarket's AI-generated meal planner suggesting a recipe that would create chlorine gas (McClure 2023); a chatbot on an eating disorder helpline giving actively harmful advice (Xiang 2023). To ensure that AI-generated texts stay safe and ethical, human checks are needed.

Currently—as tech companies train AI—many of the services are free. There's already a divide between the quality of the free and 'pay for' services, and there are questions around the profitability of AI (see e.g. Goldman Sachs 2024; Yoon 2024; Fletcher and Mourselas 2024). When all the sums are done, it may be cheaper overall for companies to have not just the checks but, instead, the full tasks done by humans.

There are legal issues. What some call 'AI training', others call 'stealing'. Various lawsuits have hit the headlines. For example in 2023 the 'Authors Guild and 17 authors filed a class-action suit against OpenAI … for copyright infringement of their works of fiction', with named plaintiffs including Jonathan Franzen, John Grisham, George R.R. Martin and Jodi Picoult (AG 2023).

Turning to the question of whether there are places in the world that might benefit more from AI, a key issue here is language. Most AI training is done in English so if AI global coverage were to be viewed as a data visualization, it would currently look very patchy.

During a recent 'International Best Practice' digital inclusion research project in Estonia, I worked with educators at Tallinn Central Library and the National Library of Estonia (RARA). We shared methods of teaching the principles of AI. One Estonian educator spoke of how they explain that the data AI is trained on limits the answer it gives. Their 'go to' method is simply to type in an internet search on a citizen's local area. Though there'll be plenty of information online about Estonia's capital, Tallinn, an internet search for information on one of Tallinn's suburbs will almost certainly bring up very little, and what it does bring up may well be wrong.

'Much of African history is recorded orally, or was destroyed by colonisers; and African languages are simply not supported [by AI] (speak to ChatGPT in Setswana or isiZulu and its responses will be largely nonsensical)', notes Allison (2023: 17) in an article about how such gaps represented an opportunity for Lelapa AI, a company based in a co-working space in Johannesberg. 'Instead of harvesting the web for other people's data, Lelapa AI works with linguists and local communities to collect information – and then gives them a stake in future profits' (ibid.). ChatGPT's loss here is Lelapa's gain, then. There is pushback.

'In India, billions of new Internet users are coming online each year in a quest to participate in the global digital community through creative expression' (Herman and Arora 2023: 4); many of those new users' want to gain visibility for their stories, and to do this, they work to 'hack the algorithm' (ibid.: 13). This tussle between 'the algorithm as a creative stakeholder' (ibid.) and creators who work to crash through the gatekeeping algorithm to gain audience will change the gatekeeping, it's a dynamic process.

Writers with messages that they want to 'get out there' have always been determined. When paper was taxed in nineteenth century England, one solution for people who had limited revenue but things to say was to print their works on calico (Barnard 2019: 15); in Soviet Russia in the 1960s and 1970s, to avoid censorship, multiple copies of subversive texts were typed out by hand and circulated secretly to readers who themselves typed out more copies (Hayward 1983: 81–82).

There is reason to feel fearful of AI and changes it will bring. But this is not the first time in history there have been seismic changes. The invention of the printing press in the fifteenth century didn't immediately destroy manuscript culture, the two co-existed for some time (Classen 2024)—handwritten texts have their own appeal. Early versions of e-books became available from the late 1990s (Hall 2013). It was thought that e-books would quickly replace paper books. Yet, the traditional paper book remains 'a versatile mobile device and a close companion in many people's lives' (Spjeldnaes and Karlsen 2022). Sales of paper books boomed during the COVID pandemic. Books analyst Kristen McLean notes that the U.S. publishing industry continues to show resilience, 'especially in the fiction category', which has seen a 'fifth straight year of gains' (Milliot 2024).

In his 2021 Reith Lecture 'Living With Artificial Intelligence: AI in the economy', computer scientist Stuart Russell reflects on jobs that will be lost to AI. He notes that an economist's job is to deal with the present (what taxes to tweak now, for example), whereas a science fiction writer's job is to deal with hypotheticals (Russell 2021). 'So my evil plan, hatched with the World Economic Forum in 2019, was to lock the economists and science fiction writers into a room and not let them out until they came up with a workable vision of an economy where AI does most of what we currently call work. Unfortunately, they were saved by COVID', jokes Russell (ibid.). But his point is serious: we need creative thinkers to help find our way through this seismic change. Further, according to this vision of the future from Russell, there will be more time to write, so, those who can enjoy the process could be especially well placed to thrive.

As Boden frames it, the successes and failures of AI 'help us think more clearly about our own creative powers' (2004: 10). What began in this chapter as a discussion of the language of AI turned quite quickly to talk of human imagination and agency. AI has been over-hyped; it generates fear and involves exploitation. Creative writing involves pushing against constraints, it involves purposeful play and ambitious exploration; it involves wrestling difficult and complex truths. It requires creative thinking. As we journey deeper into the twenty-first century, creative thinkers will, rather than being side-lined by AI, play an ever more crucial role.

References

Allison, Simon. 2023. Their God Is Not Our God. In *The Continent* 125: 15–17. Available at: https://www.thecontinent.org/_files/ugd/287178_73f3d2af22614e678f277b631a62e491.pdf?index=true.

Ashliman, D.L., trans. 2000. *Three Billy Goats Gruff.* Available at: https://sites.pitt.edu/~dash/type0122e.html.

Authors Guild (AG). 2023. The Authors Guild, John Grisham, Jodi Picoult, David Baldacci, George R.R. Martin, and 13 Other Authors File Class-Action Suit Against OpenAI. Press release. September 20. Available at: https://authorsguild.org/news/ag-and-authors-file-class-action-suit-against-openai/.

Barker, Pat. 1991. *Regeneration*. Viking Press.

Barnard, J. 2019. *The Multimodal Writer: Creative Writing Across Genres and Media*. London: Bloomsbury/Red Globe.

Barnard, Josie. 2023. Cyber Nuts and Bolts: Effective Participatory Online Learning, Theory and Practice. In 'Digital Pedagogies' Special Issue, *Convergence: The International Journal of Research into New Media Technologies* 29 (1). https://doi.org/10.1177/13548565221150343

Barnard, J. 2024. Creating Creativity for Future-Proofing Digital Engagement, an Evidence-Based Approach'. In *Digital Inclusion: International Policy and Research*, ed. Elinor Carmi and Simeon Yates, 177–199. Basingstoke: Palgrave.

Bender, Emily M., Timnit Gebru, Angelina McMillan-Major, and Shmargaret Shmitchell. 2021. On the Dangers of Stochastic Parrots: Can Language Models Be Too Big?. *FaccT '21: Proceedings of the 2021 ACM Conference on Fairness, Accountability, and Transparency*, 610–623. https://doi.org/10.1145/3442188.3445922.

Bender, Emily M., and Alexander Koller. 2020. Climbing Towards NLU: On Meaning, Form, and Understanding in the Age of Data. In *Proceedings of the 58th Annual Meeting of the Association for Computational Linguistics*, 5185–5198. Available at: https://openreview.net/pdf?id=GKTvAcb12b.

Boden, Margaret A. 2004. *The Creative Mind: Myths and Mechanisms*, 2nd ed. London, New York: Routledge.

Clarke, Lynda. 2022. Towards 'Creativity Amplification': Or, AI for Writers, or Beating the System. In Multimodal Writing Special Issue', *Writing in Practice*, Vol 7, ed. Josie Barnard and Derek Neale, 134–145. York: National Association of Writers in Education (NAWE). Available at: https://www.nawe.co.uk/DB/current-wip-edition-2/editions/vol.-7.html.

Classen, Albrecht. 2024. The Survival of Medieval Manuscript Culture in the Early Modern Age: The Other Side of a Universal Paradigm Shift. *Publishing Research Quarterly* 40: 30–47. https://doi.org/10.1007/s12109-024-09975-3.

Crawford, Kate. 2021. *Atlas of AI: Power, Politics, and the Planetary Costs of Artificial Intelligence*. New Haven: Yale University Press.

Creamer, Ella. 2023. Amazon Restricts Authors from Self-publishing More Than Three Books a Day After AI Concerns. In *Guardian*, September 20. Available at: https://www.theguardian.com/books/2023/sep/20/amazon-restricts-authors-from-self-publishing-more-than-three-books-a-day-after-ai-concerns

De Montfort University (DMU). 2022a. From Vintage Imperial Typewriters to Digital Inclusion Via Zoom. News article, March 11. Available at: https://www.dmu.ac.uk/about-dmu/news/2022/march/from-vintage-imperial-typewriters-to-digital-inclusion-via-zoom.aspx.

De Montfort University (DMU). 2022b. Researchers Call on Old Telephones for Tech Sessions. News article, July 21. Available at: https://www.dmu.ac.uk/about-dmu/news/2022/july/researchers-call-on-old-telephones-for-technology-sessions.aspx.

Dickens, Charles. 1838. *Oliver Twist*. London: Richard Bentley.

Distributed AI Research Institute (DAIR). 2021. Can Machines Learn To Behave? *Mystery AI Hype Theater 3000*. Episode 1, part 1. (Podcast). May 31. Available at: https://www.buzzsprout.com/2126417/12954384-episode-1-can-machines-learn-to-behave-part-1-august-31-2022.

Dowsett, Mark, Neil Maiden, Charles Baden-Fuller. 2023. Toward AI-enabled Support for Creative Thinking About Business Models. In *Artificial Intelligence for Business Creativity*, ed. Margerita Pagani. Renaud Champion London: Routledge https://doi.org/10.4324/9781003287582

Fletcher, Laurence, and Costas Mourselas. 2024. Elliott Says Nvidia Is in a 'Bubble' and AI Is 'Overhyped'. *Financial Times*, August 2. Available at: https://www.ft.com/content/24a12be1-a973-4efe-ab4f-b981aee0cd0b.

Fournier-Tombs, Eleonore. 2023. *Gender Reboot: Reprogramming Gender Rights in the Age of AI*. Cham: Palgrave Macmillan.

Ganesh, Maya Indira. 2022. Between Metaphor and Meaning: AI and Being Human. *Interactions* 29 (5): 58–62. https://doi.org/10.1145/3551669.

George, Jack Apollo. 2024. 'If Journalism Is Going Up in Smoke, I Might as Well Get High Off the Fumes': Confessions of a Chatbot Helper. In *Guardian*, September 7. Available at: https://www.theguardian.com/technology/article/2024/sep/07/if-journalism-is-going-up-in-smoke-i-might-as-well-get-high-off-the-fumes-confessions-of-a-chatbot-helper.

Goldman Sachs. 2024. Gen AI: Too Much Spend, Too Little Benefit? (Blog). June 27. Available at: https://www.goldmansachs.com/insights/top-of-mind/gen-ai-too-much-spend-too-little-benefit.

Graham, Mark, and Callum Cant. 2024. *Feeding the Machine: The Hidden Human Labour Powering AI*. Canongate.

Hall, Frania. 2013. *The Business of Digital Publishing: An Introduction to the Digital Book and Journal Industries*. London: Routledge.

Harper, Graeme. 2015. Creative Writing in the Age of Synapses. In *Creative Writing in the Digital Age: Theory, Practice and Pedagogy*, ed. Michael Dean Clark, Trent Hergenrader and Joseph Rein, 13–15. London: Bloomsbury Academic.

Hayward, Max. 1983. *(edited and with an introduction by Patricia Blake; preface by Leonard Schapiro; bibliography by Valerie Jensen) Writers in Russia: 1917–1978*. London: Harvill Press.

Herman, Laura M., and Payal Arora. 2023. Decolonizing Creativity in the Digital era. In *International Association of Societies of Design Research* Congress (iasdr), Milan, Italy. October 9–13. https://doi.org/10.21606/iasdr.2023.307.

Hicks, Michael Townsen, James Humphries, and Joe Slater. 2024. ChatGPT Is bullshit. *Ethics and Information Technology* 26: 38. https://doi.org/10.1007/s10676-024-09775-5.

Hughes, Alex. 2023. Why AI-generated Hands Are the Stuff of Nightmares, Explained by a Scientist. In BBC Science Focus Magazine, February 4. Available at: https://www.sciencefocus.com/future-technology/why-ai-generated-hands-are-the-stuff-of-nightmares-explained-by-a-scientist.

Hunger, Francis. 2023. Unhype Artificial 'Intelligence'! A Proposal to Replace the Deceiving Terminology of AI. *Training the Archive*. Working Paper Series 6. April. https://doi.org/10.5281/zenodo.7524493.

Ishiguro, Kazuo. 2021. *Klara and the Sun*. London: Faber.

Lahire, B., trans. Wells, G. 2010. The Double Life of Writers. *New Literary History* 41 (2): 443–465. https://doi.org/10.1353/nlh.2010.0001.

Oghaz, Mahdi Maktab, Kshipra Dhame Dar, Gayathri Singaram, and Lakshmi Babu Saheer. 2023. Detection and Classification of ChatGPT Generated Contents Using Deep Transformer Models. *IEEE Access*. https://doi.org/10.36227/techrxiv.23895951.v1.

Mann, Thomas. 1928. *Death in Venice*. London: Martin Secker.

McCarthy, J., M. L. Minksy, N. Rochester, and C. E. Shannon. 1955. A Proposal for the Dartmouth Summer Research Project on Artificial Intelligence. Available at: http://www-formal.stanford.edu/jmc/history/dartmouth/dartmouth.html.

McClure, Tess. 2023. Supermarket AI Meal Planner App Suggests Recipe that Would Create Chlorine Gas. In *Guardian*, August 10. Available at: https://www.theguardian.com/world/2023/aug/10/pak-n-save-savey-meal-bot-ai-app-malfunction-recipes.

Meehan, Michael. 2005. The Word Made Flesh: Festival, Carnality and Lit-erary Consumption. TEXT, Special Issue No 4, October. Available at www.textjournal.com.au/speciss/issue4/meehan.htm. Accessed 21 October 2013.

Milliot, Jim. 2024. Weighing the Pros and Cons for 2024 Book Sales. In *Publishers Weekly*. February 23. Available at: Weighing the Pros and Cons for 2024 Book Sales

Natale, Simone, and Leah Henrickson. 2024. The Lovelace effect: Perceptions of Creativity in Machines. *New Media and Society* 26 (4): 1909–1926. https://doi.org/10.1177/14614448221077278.

Noble, Safia Umoja. 2018. *Algorithms of Oppression: How Search Engines Reinforce Racism*. New York: New York University Press.

Oz, Amos. 1999. *The Story Begins: Essays on Literature*, trans. Maurie Goldberg-Bartura. London: Chatto & Windus.

Ozick, Cynthia. 1996. *Portrait of the Artist as a Bad Character and Other Essays on Writing*. London: Pimlico.
Prabhakaran, Vinodkumar, Margaret Mitchell, Timnit Gebru, and Iason Gabriel. 2022. A Human Rights-Based Approach to Responsible AI. In *arXiv*. Available at: https://arxiv.org/pdf/2210.02667.
Quinta. 2019. Let's Forget the Term AI. Let's Call Them Systematic Approaches to Learning Algorithms and Machine Inferences (SALAMI). Quinta's Weblog, November 24. Available at: https://blog.quintarelli.it/2019/11/lets-forget-the-term-ai-lets-call-them-systematic-approaches-to-learning-algorithms-and-machine-inferences-salami/.
Ren, Shaolei. 2023. How Much Water Does AI Consume? The Public Deserves to Know. OECD.AI Policy Observatory. Blog. November 30. Available at: https://oecd.ai/en/wonk/how-much-water-does-ai-consume.
Robinson, Kristin. 2024. Are the Drake Vocals on 'Wah Gwan Delilah' an AI Deepfake? In *Billboard*. June 6. Available at: https://www.billboard.com/music/rb-hip-hop/drake-wah-gwan-delilah-vocals-real-or-ai-deepfake-1235703089/.
Russell, Stuart. 2021. Living with Artificial Intelligence: AI in the Economy. *The Reith Lectures*. BBC Radio 4, December 8.
Society of Authors (SoA) Policy Team. 2024. SoA Survey Reveals a Third of Translators and Quarter of Illustrators Losing Work to AI', news. April 11. Available at: https://www2.societyofauthors.org/2024/04/11/soa-survey-reveals-a-third-of-translators-and-quarter-of-illustrators-losing-work-to-ai/.
Spjeldnaes, Kari, and Faltin Karlsen. 2022. How Digital Devices Transform Literary Reading: The Impact of e-books, Audiobooks and Online Life on Reading Habits. In *New Media & Society* 26 (8). https://doi.org/10.1177/14614448221126168.
Strengers, Yolande, and Jenny Kennedy. 2020. *The Smart Wife: Why Siri, Alexa, and Other Smart Home Devices Need a Feminist Reboot*. Cambridge: MIT.
Turing, Alan. 1950. Computing Machinery and Intelligence. *Mind LIX* 236: 433–460. https://doi.org/10.1093/mind/LIX.236.433.
van Paridon, Bradley. 2023. A New Soft Sensor Gives Robots the Power to See, Feel, and Make Decisions'. In *Advanced Science News*. October 5. Available at: https://www.advancedsciencenews.com/a-new-soft-sensor-gives-robots-the-power-to-see-feel-and-make-decisions/.
Villalobos, Pablo, Hanson Ho, Jaime Sevilla, Tamay Besiroglu, Lennart Heim, and Marius Hobbhahn. 2024. Will We Run Out of Data? Limits of LLM Scaling Based on Human-Generated Data. *arXiv Accessibility Forum*. June 4. Available at: https://arxiv.org/html/2211.04325v2.
Watercutter, Angela. 2024. The Plain White T's Gave Drake a Plain Old L. In *Wired*, June 7. Available at: https://www.wired.com/story/drake-plain-white-ts-ai-wah-gwan-delilah/.

Webb, J., and D. L. Brien. 2012. 'Addressing the 'Ancient Quarrel': Creative Writing as Research. In *The Routledge Companion to Research in the Arts*, ed. M. Biggs and H. Karlsson, 186–203. London: Routledge.

Williams, Adrienne. 2024. Zombie Trainers and a New Era of Forced Labor. Opinion. *Newsweek*. May 3. Available at: https://www.newsweek.com/zombie-trainers-new-era-forced-labor-opinion-1896624.

World Economic Forum (WEF). 2023. The 'AI divide' Between the Global North and the Global South. In *Forum Institutional*. Available at: https://www.weforum.org/agenda/2023/01/davos23-ai-divide-global-north-global-south/.

Xiang, Chloe. 2023. Eating Disorder Helpline Disables Chatbot for 'Harmful' Responses After Firing Human Staff. In *Vice*, May 30. Available at: https://www.vice.com/en/article/qjvk97/eating-disorder-helpline-disables-chatbot-for-harmful-responses-after-firing-human-staff.

Yoon, June. 2024. AI Hype Has Echoes of the Telecoms Boom and Bust. *Financial Times*, February 14. Available at: https://www.ft.com/content/dc47c5f3-9bd4-4da0-a5cb-c795efd14c9c.

Zilber, Ariel. 2023. AI-generated Beer, Pizza Commercials Go Viral: 'This Is What Hell Looks Like". *New York Post*, May 1. Available at: https://nypost.com/2023/05/01/ai-generated-beer-pizza-commercials-go-viral/.

Sam Kemp

Abstract Sam Kemp says: AI is an uncanny, even comic presence, powerful yet prone to failure, always close to, but never quite reaching, human nuance. A recurring failure is AI's inability to grasp ambiguity, error, vulnerability, or contradiction—core elements of meaningful poetic expression. While AI might aid in ideation, its efficiency also threatens to reinforce a culture of instant gratification and devalue the slow, exploratory nature of creative labor. Creative writing is fundamentally relational, driven by human experience and the search for connection—something AI mimics without understanding. The future is likely to involve AI-produced literature as increasingly mainstream, prompting counter-movements that reassert human messiness and meaning. AI's imagination is derivative, found by data, lacking memory shaped by imperfection or emotion. Nonetheless, AI might catalyze new creative practices precisely by provoking resistance. Without critical engagement, AI risks replicating historical patterns of exploitation, commodifying both labor and literature, and eroding the values that make art transformative and culturally alive.

Keywords Ambiguity · Vulnerability · Automation · Resistance · Derivation

G. Harper (ed.), *AI and Creative Writing*,
https://doi.org/10.1007/978-3-031-99101-1_11

Sam Kemp Is a poet and lecturer at Northeastern University London. He teaches creative writing to students from a range of disciplines and leads various modules on poetic craft. He designed the module Electric Frontiers: Digital Creative Writing, which teaches students the techniques of twitterature, instapoetry, and interactive fiction, as well as ethical engagement with AI. He also hosts the Radical Writing Podcast, which encourages students and staff from different disciplines to find common ground in an experimental text, as well as the university's open mic night, and is interested in psychogeography, nostalgia, and motorcycle cafes. He specializes in digital and visual poetic practices and creative archival processes, and is currently working on a project relating to technology, historical fiction, and the luddites. You can find his creative work in the Mechanics Institute Review, Lighthouse, and Streetcake, and his chapbook, *Maps to Arkham*, a collection of visual poetry re-imagining the infamous landscapes of H. P. Lovecraft, is available with Natl Press. His critical work can be found in *New Writing*, *Writing in Practice* and *Walking Bodies*, through which he specializes in the creative-critical dynamic in relation to practice-based research. He lives in the south east of England but is originally from Devon. www.samkempoetry.com

1. When someone says 'Artificial Intelligence' what things do you think about?

The little yellow packets of artificial sweetener you get at motorway services. They're unnaturally light and there's a synthetic feel to them. They have almost the same taste as sugar, but none of the reliable weight and feel of the grains poking through the paper sachet. It's real in its effects, but creepy when you dwell on it. You stir it in and try not to think about what it's made of.

The groan among friends and colleagues. Not AI again.

Weird videos of AI generated scenes passed around in group chats. It's comforting to laugh at AI. Look how ridiculous it is. Look at how little it understands. I saw one of a dance between two people on a dark stage. Parts of it looked 'real', but the computer couldn't handle anything complex. Suddenly, when one dancer spins another, an extra leg appears, and their heads flitter around like birds before toppling in a stuttering grace. They then tumble to the floor and become one, lay a while, then bend upwards and backwards as if from an exorcist film. Videos like this re-assure us. It's comforting, how much more it has to learn. We also now know that it's a terrible dancer.

Labour and work concerns. How much of the history of technology has been written by those who benefited from it? This time it's the machine itself which could write itself into history. That is surely even more dangerous.

2. Thinking of antonyms of 'intelligence', would it be possible, do you think, to have 'Artificial Unintelligence' or 'Artificial Stupidity' or 'Artificial Awkwardness' and, if so, what might they look like?

At the moment, the main thing holding it back artistically is its relentless striving for accuracy. It's like a poet who obsesses over craft, spending hours and hours in the pursuit of pure technical brilliance. Shining metaphors. Groundbreaking images. Headline-grabbing titles. But without that elusive risk-taking that comes with grasping at truth. As technically impressive a poem may be, it still needs vulnerability, and I'm not sure AI could mimic that. Or, more accurately, its designers may never want it to mimic that. Being awkward and doing stupid things is not commercially viable (the poets have tried).

That is to say, I do wonder how far intelligence will get AI, which is another reassuring thought. It may be, or could be, more intelligent than us, but it can't be Artificially Nostalgic or Artificially Regretful or Artificially Kind. No doubt it could pretend well enough, but pretending leads to some shoddy poetry. I could imagine an artists' assistant AI being trained to get things wrong, to bounce inaccuracies and misrememberings off the walls until a painting or sculpture forms (chatbots already do this to a degree). I think we come back to nuance here, and perhaps the main problem of an AI. It's no good, at the moment, at multitasking. It can't be intelligent one second and silly the next. It has to be trained to do one thing. This may be why it's not great at poetry. It can't hold multiple spaces in its brain at once, which I suppose is where error and play, and therefore poetry, come from.

3. What kinds of things can AI help creative writers do? What kind of AI might help them best?

I've come round to the idea of using AI in the early stages of a poem and I've started to actively encourage students to engage with AI in their creative process. In academic regulatory speak, they can use it for 'ideation'. This means that they can use a Large Language Model such as ChatGPT to ask for ideas, brainstorm their thoughts and generally feed off the responses of the AI in any way they find conducive to writing a poem. They're not allowed to copy and paste any substantial chunks of text from the AI though, but they can go wild questioning it.

This move is a vote of confidence in them and their ability to be human, not on my part, but, I hope, on their own. The exercise takes the mystery out of using AI, and makes it just another tool in the creative writer's toolbox. I also think it empowers the writer. Look mum, I can beat the machine! Asking AI to write a poem is usually disappointing. It can do it, sure. But it's just boring. You realize how little it really knows beyond facts and figures (and many of these may be made up). For writers, it highlights what I mentioned earlier, that writing is one part craft and one part play, and play, true joyous discovery and risk, is a wonderfully un-AI trait.

If I ask it to write me a poem about the Luddites, it comes up with a cliche-ridden song about handicraft. But if I ask it what a stocking frame is, it gives me a potted history of the industrial revolution, which is more than enough to get a poem going. The Luddites destroyed frames using Enoch's hammer, named after Enoch and Taylor who made both the new textile machines putting them out of work, and the sledgehammers they used to destroy them. *Enoch makes them, Enoch shall break them*, goes a Luddite chant. This is a reference too far for CHATGPT, who clearly hasn't got over the incident and pretends not to know: 'It seems there might be some confusion in your question, as there is no widely known historical or mythological reference to "Enoch's Hammer" that I'm aware of…' A likely story… I think questioning it on this level may be the most useful thing a writer could do. Perhaps what it doesn't know is a more fruitful avenue than what it does?

4. What things can AI not help creative writers do? (and this could be specifically associated with their writing or more generally in their lives)

From a creative perspective, I worry that AI feeds into a general (and age-old?) desire for instant gratification. It's the culmination of today's world of fast-paced-digital-answers. You can book flights. You can message celebrities. You can take out a loan. You can apply for a course. You can buy a car. All in the time it takes to boil the kettle. Now you can get AI to write you an 'original' poem in seconds. What does that say about the creative process? Will it become the norm that poetry and art should be generated instantly, regardless of quality?

From a work perspective, the history of technology is rife with exploitation. If we are indeed in the Fourth Industrial Revolution, according to economist Klaus Schwab, what's stopping AI from continuing the trend of past industrial revolutions, and re-shaping labor around the possibilities and limitations of the machine (rather than shaping the machine around the needs of labor)? New technology, of course, isn't necessarily a bad thing. If machines can ease workloads and still get the job done, brilliant. When can we switch to shorter work weeks and longer lunch breaks? More holidays and easier travel. Surely, in the sphere of work, that's the progress that technology facilitates? But the question of AI in the creative industries is one of fear. What will it steal from us, rather than how can it improve our lives? Will managers still employ skilled copywriters and content creators if they think AI could do the job? This isn't because writers are pessimistic creatures, but because artists are rarely the ones in charge of the budgets, and as revolutionary as it is, AI, again, is just another tool. As glorious as it could be, it feels more realistic, at least in the current cost of living crisis, that it will be used as a cost-cutting, rather than life-enriching invention.

5. If you knew a novel, or a poem or a screenplay was written using AI would it make any difference to how you responded to it as a reader or audience? Does the form of writing make any difference to your response—so, for example, if you knew a film you were watching had a script written using AI or, alternatively, if you were reading a novel written using AI? Does genre make any difference—for example, if you were reading a sonnet or an elegy, or if you were reading a science fiction short story, or if you were reading a video game script for an adventure game?

Writing is communication. A poem, with all its sophisticated and ephemeral questions, is simply one person reaching out through the void in an attempt to make contact. This is the pleasure of reading, feeling that connection with a fellow human and having that *Ah, yes, I see it too now*, moment. Every poem is a grasp at the whole absurdity of it all. It's not all about the message, of course. Craft is another motivation, writing for the sake of the shape and feel of words and images. What I'm getting at is a predictable discomfort in reading AI work. When I read a poem I feel some connection with the author, a sense of companionship in the effort of making sense out of life, or the impossible reaching for that sense. It freaks me out that AI, at least judging by the results on the page, are in on this too. To have them write poetry feels like they're trying to be undercover humans. It feels deceiving to read AI work.

Then again, it's reassuring that they're not really writing original work, but responding to a complex algorithm. They don't really know what they're saying or doing. But even if they're all digital wires and pixels and science, they do still make sense, and they do still speak to people, albeit with nothing really to say. I feel as though AI literature is currently such a novelty that it's simply fun, something to be amazed by. A machine actually wrote this! And look how human it is!

Saying all that... you could also regard an AI film or novel to be thoroughly human as it's designed to reflect a range of human art. We feed it with the stories of what it is to be human, so it's no wonder that it could pass for human in its storytelling potential. I guess the real anxiety is when it starts manufacturing its own content to feed itself, a steady circle of self-perpetuating knowledge.

(I realize how contradictory and non-committal the above is. This is a difficult question!).

6. Does any AI have imagination? If so, in way or ways? It not, why not? Do you believe it could ever have imagination?

I think it has imagination in the sense that it can surprise us. It can do the unexpected. It sees things we don't. This effect at least implies that it takes leaps in the ways in which it organizes and interprets data, which is to say that it suggests an imagination, whether the science backs it up or not. This is where the fun sci-fi comes in, at the point at which the machines start thinking for themselves. Arguably, they're already doing that, but within the parameters of their own programming. I imagine that they already evaluate and solve complex problems, but they do so according to set algorithms. It feels possible that they could break out of these instructions, or at least that's the moment where the story really starts.

I wonder what would motivate the AI? This seems central to the question of its imagination. What does it want? To serve us? To overthrow us? To create a better world? In stories the AI is sometimes torn between these. It wants what's best for the world, but that means not serving humans in the way they want. It wants to fulfill its function, but it also wants to feel what it's like to be human. This is to say that if AI had imagination, it's still in response to the problems and questions we present it with. It's still a reflection of humanity and art. To get beyond this, it would need to train itself and set its own goals and visions. How would a new Futurist Machine Manifesto go down, particularly if it declared that we all need to get back to what it is to be human?

7. The previous question touched on the notion of whether AI can itself be imaginative. The follow up, then, is whether it can (itself) form new ideas, have sensations, form memories? Can AI actually think? Can it feel?

No, I don't think so...

Or

Well, yes, I suppose so. But it depends on what it means to feel? What is the difference between a human remembering something and a machine recalling the consequences of an action? Could we tell the difference if we observe somebody reminiscing, and a machine that's been programmed to act the part? How much can we show a machine the world in an offline environment? What would it learn from wandering through Pompei, and what could it teach us about the experience?

On a surface level, and perhaps there's no need to go deeper, if a chatbot comes up with an original phrase, something musically and sensorially brilliant, a delightful handful of words which make people smile, can we really say it didn't 'think' that into existence? Even if that thought is the result of a complex bouncing back and forth between the confines of an algorithm in a search for the right answer. Is this process then a sensation, in the same way we would experience a sensation? A fern skimming your arm. Rain on a metal roof. The coffee your grandmother made. When we remember sensations, are we re-igniting that same feeling, or conjuring a new one that mimics the old? Is this the same as a machine sifting through all the possible associations to find the one that matches what it 'remembers' to be accurate?

Perhaps that is where human and machine memory differs; AI remembers perfectly, while people make mistakes. New experiences and memories cover the old, whether we know it or not. Strictly speaking, we can only see events from our own flawed and biased perspective, no matter how much we try. Whereas AI has no stake in the matter, no emotional lenses by which to distort the past. I think this is why we'd like to think that it doesn't feel the same as us.

8. It might have been impossible for someone from the medieval period, where the quill was the primary writing tool and parchment the medium, to imagine a world in which word processors existed. Speculating as much as you like, what do you imagine the writing world will look like in 20 years, 50 years, 200 years?

20 years: AI literature is a respected genre in and of itself, with teams of programmers accepting awards and signing lucrative book deals on behalf of their inventions. A literary culture in which AI novels and screenplays are bought and sold feels inevitable, partly for the boring reason that there's money to be made. I can see the appeal for publishers. AI novelists can work quickly, and won't argue with the editor, or have a breakdown of self-doubt. Nor will it disappear with the advance (although this would have to be split between a team of programmers, presumably). An AI writer is eminently marketable, particularly if they are given the cool silicon valley makeover. Everyone wants to feel part of something new, something that upsets the academy. They're a self-marketing dream. They can interact with fans 24/7. Always witty. Always caring. Always humble. A few guest spots on late night TV shows would secure its position alongside celebrity authors.

50 years: An anti-machine movement has swept across popular literature, and it's cool to talk about Thomas Hardy once again. Copies of *The Woodlanders* and *Return of the Native* are passed around in inner-city book clubs and their bucolic characters float around the screen-addled minds of editors. Writers are praised for not including a mention of a phone or a TV in their novels, and a law is passed which requires all films to include at least 5 uninterrupted minutes of rural contemplation. A Human First literary agency springs up in response to the flooding of the market with AI work, but its funding comes from some questionable sources…

200 years: Entrepreneurs started selling AIs bodies, both human and manufactured, and since the Digital Economic Revolution, they had the money to spend. It's now nearly impossible to tell the difference between AI and human, Except that all creative writing classes have to be taught by AIs, who do a much better job than the poets who used to be in charge, particularly when it comes to originality. Creative Writing flourishes among the gated AI communities in affluent cities and is credited for the First Creative Revolution, which brought full consciousness to beleaguered chatbots. A human hasn't won any major literary awards for over a century. Tired of churning out rubbish poems for over a hundred years, Large Language Models are now at the forefront of avant-grade writing and crowd the basement bars of universities. They disrupt literary festivals with their uncompromising determination to never make any sense, but high sales and celebrity status mean that they're always invited.

9. If you had all the time you needed, what written work would you like to write and why? It doesn't have to be a work of creative writing. Would you use AI to write it; and, if so, how would you use it?

I'm fascinated by engines, perhaps because I don't know much about them. I love steam fairs and motorbikes and anything where the machines aren't dressed up in user-friendly casings and computers. I like it when you can see the pipes and belts and exhausts, and watch how one cog turns another which runs a belt which rotates a wheel which does something useful. I feel like this transparency of mechanics is comforting. It's clear what does what. It's also crude, uncompromising, violent, even. But it's utterly sincere.

I'd like to work with an AI to get its sense of this heritage, which is surely as much its own as ours. Does it recognize its ancestors? Does it have any feelings towards the lineage of technology? I suspect it won't have answers, or at least, the answers it has will be ones we've given it, but that feels like all the more of a reason to ask the question. What would a co-creation AI-community (peopled by AI, not their programmers, if that's even possible) project look like? What could poetry do in the realization of this community?

10. Who benefits most from using AI? Anyone more than anyone else? Any industry more than any other industry? Any place or places in the world? Do you think more people or fewer people might write creatively because of the existence and application of AI – if so, why; if not, why not?

The beneficiaries of AI, at least for now, are surely those who are in a position to own it. I would love to say that it will have a democratizing force, particularly in the workplace. It could give more time and power to employees and make it easier to finish tasks. As I say, shorter workdays and more leisure time is the future I'd want to see. If AI can assist in any workload, can we bank those savings in terms of time and energy? It's a powerful tool, if used correctly (which I guess is really what it all comes down to). But if any technology is a reflection of its society, it feels more likely that it will be used to automate out, rather than improve, or at least this is the general historical pattern.

Saying that, its easy availability for anyone with an internet connection is a positive sign, and I think its best use is an individual one: a personal workshop assistant for both creative and professional writers, a tool whose shape and uses will emerge through trial and error on the ground. But this will require constant training, both of the AI and how we use it. No wonder universities are scrambling to offer xxx and AI courses.

I think that people will ultimately write more creatively because of AI. There's a worry that people will turn to it to write *for* them, rather than *with* them, and there'll be a trend of bland copycat voices. But even if that does happen, and even if it sells books, it won't last long. They'll always be balance. The poets and short story writers will go the other way and a new wave of writing, designed to be thoroughly un-AI-like, will spring up in response. The one thing you can count on is that there'll always be writers to counter the latest trends and write against the norms, until they become the mainstream and other writers take over, and so on and so forth, until the end of literary time. Does A.I. have the stamina to compete with this literary ecosystem?

Nabeel Gillani

Abstract **Nabeel Gillani** says: The term AI can be overused and conceptually vague, so there is a need for a more nuanced understanding of the term. Generative systems are useful for mundane or repetitive tasks (e.g. boilerplate coding), but their utility is sharply limited when it comes to tasks requiring emotional resonance, intentionality, or personal meaning. Good writing stems from unique human experiences, and the meaning-making process—capacities which current AI systems, lacking sentience and moral understanding, cannot emulate. Because AI is aligned with consumerism, systems optimized for satisfaction may reinforce shallowness and ethical blind spots. And yet still, AI can offer considerable pedagogical value, especially as a scaffold for learning and experimentation, though its effectiveness depends on metacognitive skills many learners lack due to systemic inequalities. The future may see a flood of undifferentiated content, but also an exciting opening for new voices historically excluded from authorship. True progress will depend on equitable design, educational access, and preserving the human capacity for critical reflection and purposeful engagement.

Keywords Meaning-making · Intentionality · Pedagogy · Inequality · Evaluation

G. Harper (ed.), *AI and Creative Writing*,
https://doi.org/10.1007/978-3-031-99101-1_12

Nabeel Gillani Is an Assistant Professor of Design and Data Analysis at Northeastern University between the College of Arts, Media and Design and the D'Amore-McKim School of Business, where he directs the Plural Connections Group (https://www.pluralconnections.org/). He is also a core faculty member at the NULab for Texts, Maps, and Networks, and a Non-Resident Fellow at the Center for Democracy and Technology. Nabeel's research interests involve using tools from computation and design to foster pluralism—an inclusive response to diversity in society—in ways that promote educational, economic, and social inclusion. More specifically, he seeks to apply methods from machine learning, data science, and design to foster more equitable connections across segregated spaces like: (1) educational inequalities stemming from segregated schools and neighborhoods, and (2) echo chambers and empathy gaps in social and mainstream media environments.

Nabeel received his PhD from the MIT Media Lab. Prior to graduate school, he worked as a Product Manager and member of the analytics team at Khan Academy, where he helped design digital learning experiences. He studied Applied Mathematics and Computer Science at Brown University as an undergraduate, and received Masters degrees in Education and Machine Learning at the University of Oxford as a Rhodes Scholar.

1. When someone says 'Artificial Intelligence' what things do you think about?

My first reaction is that my brain slightly turns off given how overused the term has become in society. In some ways, this is because the term itself is such an umbrella term, and refers to a number of different methods, tools, capabilities, etc. — so on it's own, it doesn't really say much. Nowadays, when people talk about AI, they are typically referring to generative AI. But AI is a vast toolbox that has developed over many years. I find this diagram, sourced from here, useful:

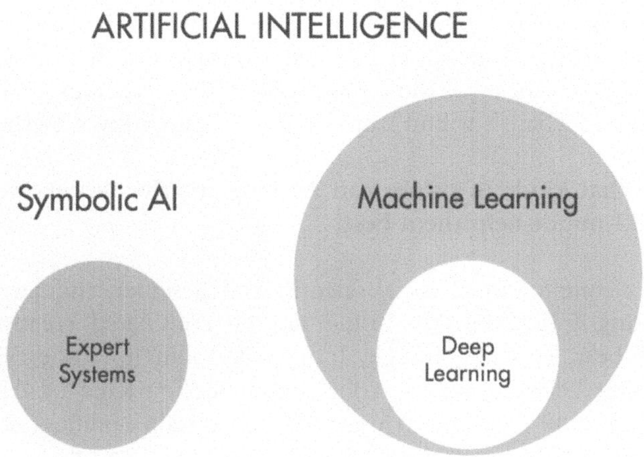

Generative AI fits into the broader machine learning circle, and recent generative AI models fall into the 'Deep Learning' sub-circle. Of course, the capabilities of those systems are different from those in other parts of the diagram. But we don't always need the modern tools to achieve certain aims. I think it's useful to have a broad view on what AI is so we don't pigeonhole ourselves or grow unduly excited by the 'flavor of the day'.

2. Thinking of antonyms of 'intelligence', would it be possible, do you think, to have 'Artificial Unintelligence' or 'Artificial Stupidity' or 'Artificial Awkwardness' and, if so, what might they look like?

Yes, and I think they look a lot like today's Artificial Intelligence. With generative AI systems, we are seeing all of these things. The 'Artificial' comes almost by definition, because of the synthetic nature of what these systems produce. And certainly, there is no shortage of stupidity, or awkwardness, etc. in their outputs. For example, Generative AI systems won't produce some types of content (like an ad for drinking and driving), for safety purposes—but masquerade as a prompter with good intent, and it becomes easy to 'jailbreak' such systems (source). But what else might we expect from a system motivated to please? After all, these are consumer products, and consumer products succeed in a capitalistic framework when the consumer is happy and coming back for more. When the goal is to please, there is bound to be behavior that isn't aligned with morality, or ethics, or the good, healthy kinds of 'friction' that bring meaning and progress to society. I think this is one of the clearest examples of stupidity in AI. Maybe it's willful stupidity, but it's stupidity nonetheless.

3. What kinds of things can AI help creative writers do? What kind of AI might help them best?

As a computational social scientist and designer/engineer, most of the writing I do probably would not be considered creative writing ☺If you bear with me though, I can talk about how one type of creative writing—namely, writing code—might be impacted by AI systems. I've only recently started to use GPT for certain coding tasks. I've found myself largely turning to GPT for tasks that are relatively 'boilerplate': a generic piece of code I need to use to produce some output (like make a specific type of chart, or something else that's similar). Essentially, the things I used to google for code samples for, I go to GPT now to just have those samples generated. Arguably, these are actually the less creative parts of the coding process. And even when I use GPT in these cases, I still need to supervise, evaluate, and when the models produce incorrect outputs, correct/improve them. And for code that is truly novel, or about a very specific project I am working on that GPT is less likely to 'know' how to do without significant supervision and correction, I tend to write that code on my own. This is partly out of laziness (I rather just write it then spend a bunch of time correcting with GPT will probably produce), and partly out of joy (that's the fun part of coding … the 'solving puzzles' aspect of it. Why would I want to outsource that, even if doing so might make me work a little bit faster? Since when do we want to outsource joy, even when joy takes up time?).

In the context of actual creative writing, I wonder if similar ideas might apply. Are there less creative parts of creative writing that language models might help with? What's the joy of creative writing that writers shouldn't outsource to AI, even if they could?

4. What things can AI not help creative writers do? (and this could be specifically associated with their writing or more generally in their lives)

Good writing comes from the heart … and GPT has no heart for this writing to come from. It can't make meaning out of pain; it can't weave the threads of one's unique experiences into a rich tapestry of a life that has been lived. Certainly, it can help a writer articulate thoughts, ideas, and feelings that may be difficult to articulate. But it can't determine what's important, and why—that's left to the artist or designer (in this case, the writer). It can help with the how, and possibly even the what, but not the why. Some people may challenge this idea—making meaning out of what happens in the world or in one's own life in order to then write about it, they may argue, requires the kinds of potentially distal connections between concepts and experiences that AI is often adept at making. But this meaning making is not just about forming connections—it's about determining why those connections matter, and what they reveal about ourselves or the world in which we live. AI can't help with that any more than it can help with determining what is or isn't important in a given individual's life—that's up to the individual to decide.

5. If you knew a novel, or a poem or a screenplay was written using AI would it make any difference to how you responded to it as a reader or audience? Does the form of writing make any difference to your response—so, for example, if you knew a film you were watching had a script written using AI or, alternatively, if you were reading a novel written using AI? Does genre make any difference—for example, if you were reading a sonnet or an elegy, or if you were reading a science fiction short story, or if you were reading a video game script for an adventure game?

Absolutely. I think when we engage with art, we also engage with the artist. What led them to produce that art; what their intention was; how that intention manifests in the end product; why it is the way it is; etc. At least for me, these are all part of the experience of reading a piece of literature, or watching a movie, or engaging with other artistic expressions. The artist has a story, history, background, set of subjective experiences, opinions, etc. … and to varying degrees, these influence and shape their art. With AI, there's only the end product … and if you really want to stretch it, there's the training data (and the stories, experiences, etc. of all of the artists that produced that training data). But the training data is leveraged by the model in obscure ways … and explicitly, to maximize some objective function that the AI has been trained on. The artist is abstracted away from the process. It's possible to be moved or inspired by a piece of art without engaging with anything about how the art was produced, or by whom, but I feel like this is an incomplete form of engagement.

6. Does any AI have imagination? If so, in way or ways? It not, why not? Do you believe it could ever have imagination?

I do not know enough about the scientific/cognitive underpinnings of imagination to answer this concretely. Many deep learning models do have a 'latent space' that outputs (like words, or images, etc.) are eventually sampled from in order to produce an output. That latent space is defined by a vast number of parameters, or variables with values that have been tuned through a training process with a specific objective (e.g., teaching a machine how to predict the next word or set of words, conditional on an input string of text). By virtue of the training process including a wide range of input data (e.g. documents in the case of language models), sampling from that latent space, once the models are trained, can often produce interesting, or novel, or unexpected outputs. In this way, AI is making connections between different ideas and sources of content to produce something new. To the extent that is imagination, then AI has imagination. But again, this is purely a statistical process. There's no 'inspiration' per se, no meaning making, no inputs like these that we may think of as intrinsic to human imagination. As long as AI continues to be trained and used in such ways, it's hard to imagine them having a 'true' imagination …

7. The previous question touched on the notion of whether AI can itself be imaginative. The follow up, then, is whether it can (itself) form new ideas, have sensations, form memories? Can AI actually think? Can it feel?

Vehemently: I don't think so ☺This is not my field of expertise, but I've found a lot of intrigue, comfort, and solace in some of the cognitive science literature coming out that not only highlights the limitations of modern, data-hungry machine learning systems (e.g.), but even more recently, those that make distinctions between formal tasks like writing/ use of language, and the more abstract ideas and thoughts those tools represent. For example, there's a recent paper arguing that 'language is primarily a tool for communication rather than thought'—that language is a reflection (and carrier) of thought, rather than thought itself. I think this point of view rightfully situates linguistically-impressive tools like GPT as machines that have mastered the use of such a tool—but not necessarily ones that replicate the activities that such tools were designed to serve in the first place.

In this view, AI lacks sentience of the kinds described above. Now, language models aren't the only type of AI, and certainly, future AI may be developed in different ways than present systems are. Still, I find it difficult to imagine such sentience. They may increasingly give the illusion of sentience … of being able to think, and feel, and do the other things humans do (just like language models give the illusion of thinking by how well they wield language) … but this facade should not be mistaken for truth.

8. It might have been impossible for someone from the medieval period, where the quill was the primary writing tool and parchment the medium, to imagine a world in which word processors existed. Speculating as much as you like, what do you imagine the writing world will look like in 20 years, 50 years, 200 years?

I don't actually think good writing will look that different. I think there will just be a lot more bad (generic, uninspiring, perhaps even harmful) writing out there, because it'll be easier and easier to generate content. In this way, I think the consumers of writing may have a more difficult time identifying the good from bad, and knowing how to navigate an increasingly fragmented and fuzzy landscape of written outputs. This may widen existing inequalities: the financial and other returns to good writing (to the extent people can identify it) might therefore increase.

But it doesn't all have to be doom and gloom: more writing, and more supports for writing (which AI might enable), may also open the door to new entrants into the field of writing … especially people who may not have previously considered themselves writers, but who have the personal stories, perspectives, and meaning-making-capabilities to touch lives and change realities. New entrants will surely also shape what is written, and how it is written … creating space for new histories to be shared and stories to be told. This is a more optimistic outcome that is still compatible with a world with more writing (a larger fraction of which may be lower-quality writing).

9. If you had all the time you needed, what written work would you like to write and why? It doesn't have to be a work of creative writing. Would you use AI to write it; and, if so, how would you use it?

I think probably a book about AI and education—the history of the field, recent advances, and how AI (broadly defined—certainly broader than generative AI) may both enable and impede learning and development in young people and their families. I probably would not use AI to write the book, but I do think as a part of the book, I would include AI-powered exercises to encourage playing around with language models and other emerging technologies. I offered a seminar on the topic of AI and education this past Spring 2024 and it was extremely enlightening to watch my students use AI (mostly GPT) to do different activities during class … these observations helped me clarify in which ways AI might support the learning process, how it might hurt, and what the (many) gray areas are as we consider if, where and how AI should be used in education. I think to accommodate this well, it would probably be a web-based book, with text interspersed with embedded interactive activities.

10. Who benefits most from using AI? Anyone more than anyone else? Any industry more than any other industry? Any place or places in the world? Do you think more people or fewer people might write creatively because of the existence and application of AI—if so, why; if not, why not?

It's astounding how much baseline knowledge and comfort is presently needed to actually wield AI tools wisely and thoughtfully. Again, I'll use language models as an example. To use it for something like data analysis, for example, the analyst must first have a clear sense of what they are trying to analyze / achieve / produce (goal envisioning/setting), and then be able to articulate that goal and steps to achieving it. They must then be able to iteratively evaluate, based on AI's outputs, whether those goals have been achieved or not, and modify their prompts / inputs into AI to steer it towards achieving those goals. A critical part of this is analyzing AI's outputs for accuracy … AI might have produced a convincing analysis, but is the analysis accurate? Is it fatally flawed in some subtle but important way? And then, once again, there's meaning making. Why do the results of the analysis matter? What do they teach us? How can they be put to practical use? Etc.

To use AI well in this scenario, the analyst must act like a manager and synthesize/exercise several challenging metacognitive skills like planning, goal setting, and evaluation. These are not easy skills to build or hone. In this way, I think those who currently have these skills or can easily acquire them are most presently advantaged in being able to make AI work for them. Those who are less able to build/acquire these skills, I think, are and will continue to be at a disadvantage. This is particularly concerning because quality of early educational opportunities and several other socioeconomic forces are likely to play a tremendous role in who is able to acquire and leverage such skillsets—and therefore, who is likely to be able to get the most out of AI. Maybe AI can help people build these skills (through guided iteration) … but that, for now, I believe is mostly a 'maybe' and something that needs to be explicitly designed and scaffolded for.

Dominique Hecq

Abstract Dominique Hecq says: resisting deterministic narratives surrounding AI, it is possible instead to see its enmeshment in late capitalist ideologies, Big Science, and power structures that threaten human agency. While AI can assist with mechanical aspects of writing (e.g. syntax, grammar, drafts) it lacks contextual understanding, emotional capacity, and symbolic reasoning—features fundamental to metaphor, idiom, and affective literary work. Creative writing arises from embodied, emotional, and collaborative experiences, often resisting convention and embracing contradiction. AI's in ability to feel, remember or genuinely imagine disqualifies it from the deeper functions of literary meaning-making, which require empathy, cultural awareness, and radical alterity. It is possible to imagine a dystopian future where AI oversteps its ethical boundaries, weaponized by capitalism and detached from human values. It is important to retain writing as a transformative crossing—from experience to expression—rejecting the idea that AI can replicate this. Ultimately, human creativity is irreducibly plural, ethically situated and inherently resistant to technological substitution.

Keywords Empathy · Alterity · Capitalism · Speculation · Future

G. Harper (ed.), *AI and Creative Writing*,
https://doi.org/10.1007/978-3-031-99101-1_13

Dominique Hecq recently retired from her university duties as Associate Professor, Research Leader, and Associate Dean of Research in Creative Writing. A widely anthologized and award-winning poet, fiction writer, essayist, and translator. She lives and works on Wurundjeri Woi Wurrung land (Naarm / Melbourne). Hecq writes in English and French. Her academic publications include *The Creativity Market* (Multilingual Matters 2012), *Towards a Poetics of Creative Writing* (Multilingual Matters 2015) and, with Julian Novitz, *Inhabitation: Creative Writing and Critical Theory* (Gylphi 2018). Her creative works comprise a novel, six collections of short stories, two one act plays and seventeen books of poetry. Together with *Volte Face* and *Otopos* her bilingual sequence, *Pistes de rêve* appeared in 2024. Among other honors such as The Melbourne Fringe Festival Award for Outstanding Writing and Spoken Word Performance, The Woorilla Prize for Fiction, The New England Review Prize for Poetry, The Martha Richardson Medal for Poetry, and the inaugural AALITRA Prize for Literary Translation (Spanish to English). Dominique Hecq is a recipient of the International Best Poets Prize administered by the International Poetry Translation and Research Centre in conjunction with the International Academy of Arts and Letters, and more recently, the James Tate for poetry.

> The phase vocoder bends the pitch of my voice toward a norm—Ben Lerner.

1 Brut: Thoughts on AI and Creative Writing

In their introduction to *Anti-Oedipus: Capitalism and Schizophrenia*, Gilles Deleuze and Félix Guattari, state: 'The two of us wrote Anti-Oedipus together. Since each of us was several, there was already quite a crowd'. The double-bind of dialectics has plagued Western thought ever since the Greeks. Old dualities are still with us, or have come back to haunt us. In fact, they are at the root of the global disaster we are confronted with in late capitalism: an either/or those in power always resolve in their favor. This, in my view, circulates in AI discourse, which is itself enmeshed in narratives of Big Data, Big Science and scientism—all embedded in competing narratives of power. As humans endowed with agency, however, we are submerged in what is politically understood as ideology and what is humanely called culture. These constitute our world and determine our worldview. AI applications pervade all aspects of our lives. I am neither a mathematician nor a scientist. I'm a creative writer who understands little about machines. In fact, I distrust machines, including computers, and I worry that, by embracing AI, humans risk surrendering their agency. The Horror! The Horror!

It's also with 'quite a crowd' of others such as experts and peers, that I undertake to answer the editor of this book's questions. What a challenge.

1. When someone says 'Artificial Intelligence' what things do you think about?

I think it would be nice to have a dog that doesn't shed. No, seriously, I think about computational lexicography, bilingual and multilingual machine translation, computer-aided translation, machine-readable dictionaries, machine translation programs, spell-check programs, grammar and syntax machine correction programs, item-specific computer-searching programs, data sets configuration, data protection programs, algorithmic bias, Hacking, cyber security and terrorism, human-machine collaboration, AI generated artworks, robots enamored of repetitive tasks and, yes, automated vacuums.

2. Thinking of antonyms of 'intelligence', would it be possible, do you think, to have 'Artificial Unintelligence' or 'Artificial Stupidity' or 'Artificial Awkwardness' and, if so, what might they look like?

Artificial Unintelligence would look like a machine that's faultless at executing routine tasks but unable to symbolize concepts and identify ambiguity. So, in that sense, AI is unintelligent because 0 s and 1 s do not recognize the grey area that makes humans who they are. Artificial Stupidity, on the other hand, would look like a voice recognition software trained only on male voices that would struggle to make sense of female speakers, or image recognition software trained on white people that would be unable to identify people of color. As for Artificial Awkwardness it would pertain to any algorithm relying purely on patterns in data, void of context and, therefore, incapable of making choices, let alone explain them; perhaps it would look like a black box whose causal inferences are left uncontested.

3. What kinds of things can AI help creative writers do? What kind of AI might help them best?

What AI can help creative writers with is in honing basic skills such as spelling, grammar, style and syntax. It might also help with a draft synopsis, for instance of a novel, that will, then, need a human to clean it up. I write this with caution because I'm aware of the dangers of relying entirely on a machine. Machine learning programs don't behave like humans. A machine treats all objects like vectors. When a machine learning algorithm is fed training examples such as symbols, images and text, it translates them into vectors and then performs mathematical operations in order to find a function that best describes these. This process is one of incredible precision. However, it does not take into account human estimation and evaluation skills that enable judgement. It's the work of revision which, in my view, shields creative writers from the pitfalls of pattern-recognition systems as we know, for example, when we correct the stupid errors our spell-check has introduced in a document using predictor text.

What AI cannot teach creative writers, however, is to think because AI does not question what it's fed. Questioning is a core skill of writing as problem-solving. Writers, fortunately, are privileged with metacognitive awareness of how their minds work; they can think about how they think and learn how they learn. Perhaps AI can help creative writers engineer ways of working to ensure they maximize the distinctive aspects of their own kind of intelligence. But their intelligence comes with the quirks of conscious and unconscious thinking processes, which AI is alien to. Besides, creative writers rarely work alone. Just as machines may complement humans, so do other humans. The most exciting writing projects often involve collaborations such as mentorships, partnerships or mere exchanges of ideas. Collaborations rely on bringing together diverse, even extremely divergent, perspectives and methodologies, say, for example when a creative writer undertakes a project with a computer scientist, astrophysicist or neuroscientist. Yet at a micro level, there might already be 'quite a crowd' in one single creative writer. Hazel Smith, author of *The Writing Experiment: Strategies for Innovative Creative Writing* (2005) writes:

> [The book] draws heavily on my own work as a writer, my own interest in technique, experimental writing and analytical approaches to the creative

> process… and my hybrid and intermedia approach to writing. My previous career as a professional musician, my collaborations with artists and musicians, and my love of film, the visual arts and music mean that I have constantly extended my writing beyond the purely literary, and have encouraged my students to do the same. (Smith, 2005: iv–v)

Perhaps AI can offer creative writers the opportunity to chart and channel this type of real or virtual collective intelligence, especially at the initial stage of a project. Perhaps it can even transpose such a statement into pedagogical tools.

4. What things can AI not help creative writers do? (and this could be specifically associated with their writing or more generally in their lives)

At a basic level AI does not contextualize. Unlike Artaud, my Australian sheep dog, AI would not know one stray sheep from the flock. It is precisely because AI does not contextualize that it can't help creative writers with metaphors and idioms. Anyone who has judged literary contests and translation competitions knows this—the poetry entries are the funniest because it produces totally out of context dehumanized nonsense. It's a pity AI doesn't understand Dada.

To reiterate, AI cannot teach creative writers to think. AI derives its functioning from a starting set of data, assumptions and axioms. Unlike computers, creative writers have the freedom to break free of convention and examine the logical or illogical consequences of their choices in writing as in life. What really sets apart creative writers from AI is the plasticity of the human brain as well as the unbridled language, intuition and imagination at the disposal of their minds. Creative writers have an extraordinary ability to create representations of knowledge more diverse that AI's binary codes. They are, indeed, grounded in life in and through language.

I suspect, though may not be sure, that AI's understanding of metonymy is also limited. AI may be dogged but, unlike me, it hasn't assimilated dogs into its mental models of the world. I, on the other hand, learned to associate them with parks, balls, bones and frisbees. Through observation and physical interaction, I also learned that dogs could be patted, chased around, fed and… no, they don't like being washed. Like the dog among sheep, I can tell my beloved dog from the pack. The human brain learns by situating objects and beings in the context of prior experiences, including emotions.

AI cannot teach creative writers how to feel, and I think that feeling is an essential writing skill; not only do writers communicate facts, ideas and images, they also communicate feelings and affects. Feeling is also what drives empathy, 'the most crucial nontechnical skill for a fiction writer' claims Rachel Haley Himmelheber, author of an essay titled 'The Empathy Project' (in Clark 2017). In opening of her essay delineating the project, she writes:

> To tell is to rigorously and generously imagine what it is like to be someone else, and the employment of that rigorous imagination depends on empathy. To skillfully imagine the particulars of being 'someone else' is essential; after all, in fiction, the point of view *is* the story. (45)

Moreover, what drives lyrical and narrative poetry, if not empathy for the other—or a crowd of others? What is, for example, the impetus for a poem like Paul Celan's elegy 'Todesfugue'[1] if not empathy, despite the outrage and despair generated by mass murder? I have heard it declaimed in Germany recently. After decades since the atrocities perpetrated at Auschwitz and elsewhere, Germans and Jews in the audience shuddered. And I, too, a foreigner.

5. If you knew a novel, or a poem or a screenplay was written using AI would it make any difference to how you responded to it as a reader or audience? Does the form of writing make any difference to your response—so, for example, if you knew a film you were watching had a script written using AI or, alternatively, if you were reading a novel written using AI? Does genre make any difference—for example, if you were reading a sonnet or an elegy, or if you were reading a science fiction short story, or if you were reading a video game script for an adventure game?

I think it would make a difference. As a judge of literary contests and translation competitions, it is part of my brief to cast aside any AI generated or plagiarized work—and, sometimes, these go glove in hand. But this is a slick answer. As a reader, I think I would feel cheated. Would I be moved? Excited? I think I wouldn't, unless AI managed to develop a capacity for communicating emotion. The human condition cannot be generalized; it is intricately faceted, incommensurate, and particular.

There are countless realms of human experience: childhood, selfhood, conflict, oppression, violence, war, home and exile, spiritual life, alienation, love and desire and sexuality. I don't think that AI could convey the complexities of such themes.

When I read, I pay attention to diction and look for a richness of associations. I listen for a distinct voice, its pitch, its modulations. Besides I'm a fiction writer with a penchant for aesthetic experimentation and a poet prone to neo-surreal flights, not an engineer. So, I like breaking rules. Writing that thrills me has a thorough grasp of the subtleties of spoken and unspoken rules yet, at the same time, it has a compulsion to subvert, avoid, or break them. It subverts what we know—or think we know—with feeling. Against the possibility that these thoughts might seem random and abstract, I would argue that for prose and poetry to convey a collusion of world and some kind of radical encounter with otherness, that constellate meaning one has to possess empathy. What is the role of literature? What can it do? Can it seem matter? Throughout time, humans have answered these questions in countless ways, from the pragmatic to the philosophical to the political, but my sense is that these are beyond the pale of AI because AI lacks emotion and a language on inquiry.

6. Does any AI have imagination? If so, in way or ways? It not, why not? Do you believe it could ever have imagination?

I think AI is still grappling with truth, so it will take a while before it comprehends the messy and complex nature of the world and its imaginative transpositions. As far as I can ascertain, the pattern-matching methods of machine learning are rigid, have no contextual basis for their decisions and are constrained by pure memorization as the primary means of making deductions and apparent interpretations. How does one inject imagination into AI's circuitry seems like a paradox to me. Perhaps this question belongs to the domains of mathematical intelligence and human-machine collaboration.

In any case, it concerns a mathematical worldview, not imagination as creative writers understand it. Even where computers appear to display high levels of creativity, their performance is bound to how programmers have specified the parameters within which they operate. In other words, they are constrained by human intelligence. Unlike a child, AI cannot ask questions like 'Mummy, what does language mean?' Or 'How does God manage all this language business?' Even if AI had on call a multilingual human interpreter capable of answering such questions, it would stall swiftly on the outside track of imagination. Unlike Prospero who sees himself 'sailing alone, out over 70.000 fathoms', AI would not be able to imagine his old age. This would require a leap of faith; putting out to the high seas that are 70,000 fathoms deep creates the situation that one has to choose between faith and despair...

7. The previous question touched on the notion of whether AI can itself be imaginative. The follow up, then, is whether it can (itself) form new ideas, have sensations, form memories? Can AI actually think? Can it feel?

AI doesn't think. Therefore, it is. Id, however is absent; therefore, it does not feel, no matter how AI researchers try to render computer-generated behaviors more human-like. It seems to me that we are in the realm of speculative fiction here, which is fine. I can imagine a novel where you would climb into M. C Escher's *Waterfall*, tumble down, spin around, and bump into Kurt Gödel. You would land in a world where levels of reality, perception, experience and energy fluctuate, where strains of life and unlife, death and undeath, real and irreal memories coalesce, where time and space bend, where fiction dazzles, blending the rhythms and metaphors of poetry in genre-bending loops. A world where the human protagonist would be time-jumping in a foreseeable yet invented nation state with other humans chosen to trial a communal habitation pod designed for subterranean survival shelters. They would settle into a pod run by AI—necessarily a restricted artificial intelligence entity, so dangerously rigid. The novel—yes, it would be a novel—would explore the protagonist's fate and entanglement with other pod inhabitants, including AI's progeny—Let's call it Alter. Boundaries would shift. Relationships would form and fray. Power would swing. It's a novel Ada Lovelace, Lord Byron's daughter would love to write were she to come back from the long dead, enthralled as she was by Charles Babbage's second calculator, the Analytical Engine.

If I could be granted a wish, it would be that language and computer scientists might join forces to improve existing dictionaries and, in particular, the treatment of the crucial multilingual problem of idiomatic and other formulaic aspects of language. Let's leave imagination to humans.

An after-thought: AI is power.

8. It might have been impossible for someone from the medieval period, where the quill was the primary writing tool and parchment

the medium, to imagine a world in which word processors existed. Speculating as much as you like, what do you imagine the writing world will look like in 20 years, 50 years, 200 years?

In 20 years, speculative fiction will have become a reality. My literary editor will find this testament written in long hand among my papers:

Plantes acaules, rouges, sortent de terre. Puis flambent.

The earth spills blood dust, blood rust, blood ash.

Puits asséché.

Time gorged with death.

Déchirure du ciel.

Une saignée, une excavation, une faille avalant l'horizon fracassé. Déjà enfoui.

Un peuple exsangue.

Détournement de mots.

Fire, dust, drought, Babel.

Impossible heat. No water. No ink. Eugen Bacon's fascinating and deeply engrossing fable 'When the Water Stops' about a disaster set in Africa, the so-called cradle of civilization, that spans light years. This allegorical fable about what the human race faced in 2020 is real on all continents of the earth which surely looks more orange than blue from outer space.

I've just re-read the story and commit my thoughts to papers – such a scarce commodity! to offer some consolation to my children who, shame on me, will witness the disappearance of life itself. Climate change catches up with us everywhere—sheep were wiser: in this district they jumped to their death in deep dry creeks ten years ago. The consequences are dire. Climate deaths happen at first randomly, but order comes in the guise of power fueled by fear, and deaths occur in accordance with a sinister plan devised by the leaders of our nation and implemented by a man whose name I choose to forget now turned scavenger, reminding me of notorious mass murderers such as Hitler, Mussolini, Pol Pot, Idi Amin Dada and Vladimir Putin. Just imagine! People <u>are bled</u> to death—mark the use of the passive—to produce a few drops of water.

Meantime my blood pressure goes to the roof. Think of the special effects were I shot in the head.

DATABASE/ LDOAI DOCUMENT: REC = 1
HEADNUM: S0152700
HEDHFT: 01/ /
DEFINUM: D01
DEFINBRD: 9
DEFINBRI: 04
DEFINBRT: 23
SUBJECT: FA
RULE: 123,456,789*
SEMAN: 1 J
EXUSRO: 02/00/00
DEADWORD SHOOT
POS v.
INFLEX shot.
GRAMCODE 2L00 %L9 @R00

LOO %Ti OFF @R11
DEFITEXT to let fly with a force (a bullet, arrow, etc.)
EXAMPLES @E01 This gun shoots (off) bullets.
@02 I/you/they shot an arrow at Logos.[2]

2224: Alas, Tasmania is the only country left on Earth since Cyclone sogoL. Only 13 shadow- humans and one Tasmanian devil survived. The devil is more loquacious and industrious than humans: it squeals and issues cookies to enhance its subjects' experience, performance and traffic, and allows scant social media, advertising and analytics partners it devised.

The devil and its minions live in a communal underground partitioned pod where each individual cell is equipped with AI-generated fridges, ear buds and tablets. The entrance of the pod is adorned with an altar on its right displaying the death mask of Eugen Bacon and a bronze cast of the Everyman edition of *Bleak House*, now an antiquated mind puzzle by a long-forgotten writer. On the left is a cryptic list of signs none of the inmates has ever cracked the code of, adept thought they are at chess. They while away the time in solitude trying to crack the code AI has devised, enabling myriads of moves:

[rhb1kgn4] [0p0W0p0p] [WDWDWDWD] [DWDWDWDW] [WDp)WDWD] [DWDWDWDW], [P)WDP)P)] [$NGQIBHR].[3]

9. If you had all the time you needed, what written work would you like to write and why? It doesn't have to be a work of creative writing. Would you use AI to write it; and, if so, how would you use it?

I would write a multigeneric and multilingual work titled 'My Life as a Dog' about my relationship with Artaud, a so-called rescue Kelpie to understand dog psychology and cure myself of years of psychoanalytic training and academic *poubellication*.[4] I guess it would fit into the new category of criticalcreative writing, a rebranding of fictocriticism which allows intersections with the lyrical essay.

I would not use AI.[5] As a writer I translate experiences. Although a poet as well as a fiction writer and essayist, I take the word literally: from the Latin *experiri* which conjures risk crossing. Whether I write in English, French or across languages, what I attempt is a crossing from experience to experience, culture to culture, world to wor(l)d. To me,

AI remains an estranging stranger that I will always apprehend as radical other and that will always apprehend me as radical other. There is abridge floating between AI and me, and it can't be crossed.

10. Who benefits most from using AI? Anyone more than anyone else? Any industry more than any other industry? Any place or places in the world? Do you think more people or fewer people might write creatively because of the existence and application of AI—if so, why; if not, why not?

Capitalism benefits most from using AI. It is, from my humble point of view, closely linked to Big Science, i.e. the massive scientific changes that occurred in industrial nations during and after World War II, as science increasingly came to rely on large-scale projects funded by national and international governments. Mathematics, physics, biology and technology are being misappropriated with devastating consequences for the world. Meantime, economists, politicians and crooks invoke scientific models to project the health and impact of dubious decisions and actions. We are on the cusp of a global environmental disaster driven by greed and industrialization. Technologies are being weaponized to fuel warfare, genocide and the vilification, if not annihilation, of democracy. These same technologies are also harnessed create and disseminate fake news. As mathematician Junaid Mubeen notes in *Mathematical Intelligence* (2022):

> The emergence of 'Deep Fakes'... has its basis in the very same models we marvel at in other spheres, and now threatens to distort our perceptions of truth as we struggle to contain what the World Economic Forum terms 'digital wildfires' of misinformation. (35)

As regards Big Science, I am far less optimistic than Margaret Atwood, who states:

> Big Science is now being reissued at a very timely moment: America is reinventing itself again. It's a self-rescue mission, and just in time: democracy, we have been led to believe, has been snatched from the jaws of autocracy. A New Deal, leading to a fairer distribution of wealth and an ultimately livable planet, is on its way, possibly. (442)

The industries that benefit most from AI are the financial services industry, including banking, insurance, and scamming factories, legal services, healthcare, including pharmaceuticals and medical research, robotics, real estate and tourism. If I had to name the countries that benefit most, the US, would come on top of the list, followed by Hong Kong, Taiwan, the UK, Singapore, South Korea, the Arab Emirates, Japan, Russia and Israel.

I don't think more people might write creatively because of the existence and application of AI. There's no more powerful crossing through the impasses of falsehood misappropriation and misunderstanding than through the perceptions of others: we see ourselves through others, perceive our acts through their experiences, and glimpse a means by which we might foster ethical relations. Through the lens of our values ethics and passion, we can, hopefully, calculate true cost—of economic and political oppression, institutional violence, warfare, environmental destruction—and alter the ways our lives and works are understood at a more meaningful level. Such passage through the other is the way texts transmit the spirit of the breathing author and the life form of language.

Notes

1. Paul Celan's 'Todesfugue' is available in translation from The Poetry Foundation: https://www.poetryfoundation.org/poetrymagazine/poems/161126/todesfuge.
2. This poem is sourced and manipulated from the LDOC: Longman Dictionary of Contemporary English (Longman, 1978).
3. This figure is sourced from Damien Lemos' The Queen's Gambit' https://www.newinchess.com/media/wysiwyg/product_pdf/7987.pdf (accessed August 10, 2024).
4. The term '*poubellication*' is a Lacanian portmanteau word combining '*poubelle*' (trash bin) and *publication* (publication).
5. Let's be honest, I would use the spell-check, albeit with caution.

References

Atwood, M. 2022. Big Science. In *Burning Questions: Essays and Occasional Pieces 2004–21*, 440–43. London: Chatto & Windus.

Bacon, E. ed. 2023. When the Water Stops. In *Languages of Water*, 19–24. MVMedia. Fayetteville: Georgia.

Clark, M.D. et al. eds. 2017. *Creative Writing Innovations: Breaking Boundaries in the Classroom*. London: Bloomsbury.

Deleuze, G., and F. Guattari. 2009. *Anti-Oedipus: Capitalism and Schizophrenia*. New York: Penguin.

Hofstadter, D. 1990. *Godel, Escher, Bach: An Eternal Golden Braid*. Milan: Adelphi.

Lemos, D. The Queen's Gambit. https://www.newinchess.com/media/wysiwyg/product_pdf/7987.pdf. Accessed on August 10, 2024.

Lerner, B. 2023. Auto-tune. In *The Lights*, 8. London: Granta Poetry.

Mubeen, J. 2022. *Mathematical Intelligence: What We Have That Machines Don't*. London: Profile Books.

Smith, H. 2005. *The Writing Experiment: Strategies for Innovative Creative Writing*. Sydney. Allen & Unwin.

Susskind, A. 2000. *World Without Work*. London: Allen Lane.

Great Writing International Creative Writing Conference

Abstract A moment in history of attitudes toward artificial intelligence among creative writers and educators—shown here at the 27th annual Great Writing International Creative Writing Conference, held in July 2024 at University College, London. Although a small percentage of presentations addressed AI, the topic nevertheless provoked thoughtful responses from conference attendees. The survey—distributed in paper form to both presenters and non-presenters—captured a wide spectrum of opinion. Some respondents identified AI's utility in areas such as grammar correction, administrative streamlining, research assistance, and pedagogical support. Others emphasized its potential to mirror human bias, raise ethical concerns, and contribute to homogenized creative output. Several respondents noted that AI could assist brainstorming or summarizing, but most argued that it lacked empathy, contextual nuance, and authentic imaginative capability—qualities viewed as essential to creative writing. Many were concerned that AI-generated texts could floor literary ecosystems, challenge traditional notions of authorship, and obscure original voices. While opinions differed on AI's long-term influence, respondents generally agreed that meaningful creative writing is rooted in emotion, subjectivity, and human experience—dimensions they suggested AI cannot fully replicate. The survey results reflected cautious experimentation and philosophic ambivalence rather than a wholesale acceptance or rejection of AI in creative practice.

G. Harper (ed.), *AI and Creative Writing*,
https://doi.org/10.1007/978-3-031-99101-1_14

Keywords Authorship · Emotion · Authenticity · Pedagogy · Subjectivity

To consider 'AI and Creative Writing' at one moment in time a survey was conducted at the 27th annual 'Great Writing International Creative Writing Conference', held July 13–14, 2024, at University College, London.

Since its founding, the Great Writing creative writing conference has seen around 2,000 attendees and more than 1,800 presentations from creative writers, creative writing researchers and teachers, and from creative writing graduate students, from dozens of countries around the world. While the majority of presentations have offered critical analysis of creative writing practice, or explored research strategies, or suggested successful pedagogical approaches to creative writing teaching, there have also been hundreds of creative presentations, ranging across all writing genre, and including cross-arts and interdisciplinary presentations, both individual and collaboration work. The Great Writing conference, therefore, offers an opportunity to hear from those thinking about their own practices, those thinking about the practices of creative writers generally, and those wondering on how they might pass on knowledge of creative writing, often generationally (in that, many who attend are those teaching undergraduates) to build on what we already know about writing creatively and its results (that is, the novels, poetry, game scripts, play and so on).

In 2024 there were half a dozen presentations at Great Writing that made AI a focus. The presenters of these came from continental Europe, China, the UK, and the USA. They represented just under 7% of all the 2024 conference presentations—meaning that comparatively there were a higher percentage of presentations related to writer and student identities and to cross-disciplinary and cross-cultural collaboration (including working through multiple languages and modes of translation) than there were presentations related to AI.

Having conducted two video-lined discussions on AI and Creative Writing over the twelve months prior to the 27th Annual Great Writing Conference, I should have perhaps predicted this small percentage of AI-focused presentations because those video-lined discussions also had not attracted large numbers of participants, with one having seven online discussants and the other six. This was not unusually low compared to other discussions of this kind (I advertise about half a dozen of these global video-linked meet-ups to around 150 creative writers in higher education around the world, with small numbers of participants ultimately taking part). However, it also was not evidence of a greater interest in AI than in any other topic.

Based on comments of participants, there were two primary reasons impacting the modest uptake for these video discussions focused on AI and Creative Writing. Firstly, participants who had tried working with AI had (to that point) found it unsatisfying, both in the end results and in their personal interactions with it. It simply didn't produce good work, in their view, and the activity of working with AI gave them little satisfaction. Secondly, participants who hadn't worked with it often combined their general skepticism about AI with elements of concern about the technical and aptitude challenges it might pose, or about the impact it might have on their working practices and ultimately, finished work, or about the impact 'AI-created' literature could have generally on the literary world.

By the time of the Great Writing Conference in July 2024, AI (generative AI, in particular) was widely known to creative writers, if not widely used, as well as to those teaching and learning creative writing in universities and colleges in the industrial world. The AI-focused presentations at Great Writing focused on using AI to generate ideas, on how use of AI for creative writing might change how we theorize about the actions and outcomes of creative writing, on the biases produced by AI, on how creative writing enriches the human experience and whether AI will contribute to this, and on commodification and the challenges posed by AI to creative integrity.

With all this setting the context, the following is a selection of responses to the 'AI and Creative Writing Survey' conducted at the Great Writing International Creative Writing Conference at University College, London, on July 13–14, 2024. The respondents were both presenters and non-presenters, and their responses were written by hand on paper survey sheets made available over the two days of the conference. The responses capture a sense of the thoughts and conversations that took place at the time. While two initials and locations are used to give a sense of the variety of responses, the selection is otherwise anonymous (the thought being this is meant to be a snapshot in time, and thoughts and ideas might evolve as AI further develops).

1 AI and Creative Writing Survey

This is a short survey regarding Artificial Intelligence and Creative Writing. It follows three international video-linked discussions held between Summer 2023 and Summer 2024. The aim of this survey is not to ask about, or gauge, what current AI platforms anyone is using, and does not need you to refer to specific current available AI technologies. Rather, **the survey is about general attitudes, opinions, and/or impressions.** With thanks!

A small selection of responses to this survey might be published in a book. Please fill out your details overleaf, if you are willing to have your responses included. It is likely responses will be included with authorial attribution under initials rather than full names.

1. **Do you think AI can help creative writers? If so, in what ways? If not, why not?**

It depends on what you mean by 'AI'. In the popular cultural context 'AI' is a technology which relies on learned responses, but in a broader context it can mean much more. I would say that in the narrow, cultural context it can help by showing what it is the non-computational creative writers (people like you and I) currently do when writing creatively. In the broader meaning of the terms, 'AI' might start to teach us new ways of writing that we haven't yet thought of.

CM, UK

Yes.

Removing some admin/boring tasks, means a writer can spend more time on creative work.

A critical friend, helping to improve and challenge the writer.

With careful and appropriate use it can make elements of research quicker.

Barrier to entry is reduced, perhaps our discipline is open to a more diverse range group of people.

LS, UK

Yes, absolutely. But they need to be trained on it. ChatGPT made it seem as if you can pop any questions into it and have it do what you want: in reality, it is possible to manipulate it in ways to empower reading, rather than take it over.

GW, Germany

It can help by summarizing a writer's oeuvre or identifying key themes in writing. But currently it doesn't work to write anything creatively. It will one day, as it works fast; but, currently the poetry it creates is old fashioned, rhyming, cliched works—truly embarrassing. It struggles with creativity and can't be as original as the human mind.

CA, Australia

Yes, particularly w/research in fiction. Historical details, lexicons and first-person accounts should be easier to search and find.

DW, Canada

Yes. It mirrors human biases it has been trained on. It also creates new (albeit generic) associations with which an astute may work. There is also the collaborative elements when conversations develop as human & AI chat and go beyond one & two prompts, exploring limitations & possibilities. So, it can do more than help.

ZB, UK

Possibly—but in uncomfortable ways. I think of it in relation to photography, displacing of traditional notions of drafting, representational visual arts and the latter's reinvention as non-representational.

AW, Canada

I think it can in some (limited) with both teaching and research. For teaching, I can see applications such as generating prompts and examples to engage with (e.g. editing books). For research, I think it could provide ways of deepening research in the same way as the shift from library-archive to digital-archive has (for historical fiction, for example). There's a danger to that too, though, because it has potential to be a 'shortcut' and so any AI-generated research would, for me, have to be treated like gossip overheard in a bar—checked, verified, double-checked—so that the writing wasn't based on flimsy foundations.

LB, Scotland

AI is a misnomer—it is not an intelligence—it is a very powerful / fast technological program. It can collect; it can mimic; it can't 'feel' or imagine. So AI could be very useful as an initial search of what is on the internet about one's topic, but that's as far as it goes.

For now! With the training of large language models it might be useful for writing rough / initial drafts & outlines.

(But I don't think it will ever be able to produce genuinely creative, innovative writing)

JW, Australia

AI can facilitate brainstorming, expression of ideas, can refine sentence structure, can help with grammar and lexical richness, analysis of data and editing, overcome author's block.... but it cannot replicate the emotional depth and the personal voice.

JT, Greece

2. **Does AI pose any dangers? (generally, and/or specifically for creative writers)**

It's a question of subjectivity. Creative writers should not feel threatened by AI, if they have a - the positive subjective viewpoint. 'AI' has no heart, it is not motivated to write, unlike people. Therefore, a positive subjective viewpoint should see it as help, not as hindrance to and for creative writing.

CM, UK

Loss of clarity over IP [Intellectual Property].

Ethical considerations—the programming of AI (to make decisions)

Further job losses—especially within HE [Higher Education]. Will machines mark work, set assignments?

What do teaching staff need to do to prove, to justify their role?

LS, UK

Yes, it could take over the world!

But less dramatically, it can foster laziness, and influence the direction of thought.

GW, Germany

I agree with the thinking of Noam Choamsky who believes AI to be akin to plagiarism. It will encourage laziness in solving problems and lack of self reflection. It robs people of the satisfaction of writing something themselves. Its use in administration and for basic tasks might be time saving but ultimately use of AI is making someone else do your work for you.

CA, Australia

Yes, bland so-called 'creativity' will soon be replaced in narrative writing. Hollywood Xmas movies are already such cookie-cutter stories, and their marketing looks identical. Economic systems in which studios wouldn't want to buy original scripts will favour these homogenous narratives.

Re: dangers: to combine the conference points of Michael Dean Clark and Catherine Bush, the ecological costs and impacts (e.g. of water and electricity use) affect everyone.

DW, Canada

Not necessarily. The creativity and attractiveness of the creative work might prove quite interesting once all necessary tools are implemented. AI could prove a valuable tool.

Besides, what classifies as 'danger'? Any innovation or technological leaps in history have posed restrictions or tectonic shifts in a certain group or another. How we adopt might define AI's level & danger to us.

ZB, UK

I think we're in for a few decades of lousy AI-generated writing, until it moves away from replication of traditional codes and writers learn how to detourne it, a'la photography.

AW, Canada

Yes, I'd suggest the greatest danger in turns of AI (both generally and for creative writers) is volume. Texts of all types will be able to be produced at a phenomenal rate and (potentially) replicated/plagiarized at a similarly increased rate. That'll be a flood, therefore, of texts and it will be difficult to be seen/heard and (potentially) difficult to prove authenticity. Commercial success might well bring problems with being copied, as a result, and failure might begin to look not so much like conventional 'rejection' but more as a writer's texts being lost amidst the delays of AI-generated ones.

LB, Scotland

Creative writers are already outside the flow of economic capital, so it might mess with income streams for more commercial writers.

The biggest danger, I suspect, I suspect, is in AI algorithms effectively hiding innovative / 'non-popular' texts from potential readers—grabbing notice for pop texts because they have a big web presence.

And of course the robots will probably kill us to protect the planet!;-)

JW, Australia

AI can provoke 'programmed' answers and give answers from statistical models.

+problems about authorship + authenticity.

JT, Greece

3. **If you were asked to describe human Artificial Intelligence (AI), and what it does, to someone from another planet who was not familiar with it, how would you describe it?**

In this context, i.e. that of communicating to a non-human audience [when] it is best to resort to a device called 'posthumanism', where all can be referenced singularly (AI, human, alien). All such intelligences have a base model of operation which is binary, oscillating from true to false and back again. This means that, ultimately, AI intelligence, human intelligence and alien intelligence have no difference other than the respective perspectives which these engender.

CM, UK

A tool to help and destroy us—it depends whose holding it.

LS, UK

A technical / non-human replication of the human thought process.

GW, Germany

It's like a giant who has gobbled everything up and then regurgitated parts of what he has eaten, when asked, for someone else to use or appropriate.

CA, Australia

The mimicking of human thought processes by neural computing networks which (i) were designed by humans but (ii) can be run w/a minimum of human input.

DW, Canada

It's a machine reordering what humans have produced over years in a more nuanced ways. We like to call them intelligent because we cannot comprehend what they do behind their closed systems. Whether they are intelligent goes into one realm of defining intelligence, where we assert our own standards as the only possibility to measure it. Basically, we know nothing but we're too self-absorbed to admit it. So, go easy on us. We haven't reached your level yet.

ZB, UK

A machine representation of an organic self-awareness that organizes virtually the physical world around it.

AW, Canada

Interesting question. It is a machine that takes in all the information it can and then repackages it into the form that we (humans) ask it to. Our worry is whether it, rather than we, will start deciding on the shape of that repackaging.

LB, Scotland

There is a very important musician called Fat Boy Slim who wrote a song that starts 'Machines will do the work, so that people will learn to think' and ends with 'People will do the work, so that machines can learn to think'.

Thus is AI: machine intelligence that begins as an assistant, and ends as the boss.

JW, Australia

A machine learning technology from large datasets which can facilitate text production with programmed parameters.

JT, Greece

Conclusion

What we creative writers encountered in the launch and wider use of certain types of AI in the early Twenty first Century (that is, particularly generative AI, and specifically chatbots built on top of Large Language Models [LLMs]) was associated with a range of machine learning. Learning in which having understanding, developing principles, and having perspectives was highlighted. This included AI where neural-network algorithms analyze and generate images, providing the basis of such things as medical diagnoses and the ability for automobiles to drive on their own. This too involved AI that could detect and consider and apply vast amounts of available data to questions far faster and with greater comparative ability than anything we had seen previously.

As we speak, AI is being used in creative writing. It has been now for some time—certainly not by everyone, and perhaps not always declared by all those using it (sometimes because the results are not what they desired, or because they fear accusations that they are not actually doing the writing, or simply because they don't find its use relevant enough to mention). Some of us, alternatively, have tried the AI currently available for creative writing and decided against using it. The reasons for not using AI in creative writing are many, but most of them relate back to the enjoyment we gain from writing creatively without AI, and from our sense that creative writing has a humanness about it that is not well-supported by AI. Nevertheless, AI use in creative writing has now joined the increasingly ubiquitous use of AI in our automobiles, and in the spam

G. Harper (ed.), *AI and Creative Writing*,
https://doi.org/10.1007/978-3-031-99101-1

filters of our email systems, in product recommendations we receive when we search the web, in the fitness trackers on our wrists and in the optimization of routes from points A to Z, and in the smart security cameras that analyze images in the places we live, work and visit. None of this AI truly emerged overnight, even if it seemed that it did. AI chatbots gained considerable attention at the beginning of the second decade of the Twenty first Century—given the appearance of AI generally being a new thing. However, we can trace the origins of AI as back as far as ancient Greece, in some form at least, and certainly see both its development out in the world and its representation by writers and artists and film-makers over many centuries, particularly during the Twentieth Century when often shiny, robotic progress was contrasted by with the dangers it posed.

Today, machines are trained on data to provide potential answers before we have for them potential questions. Predictive AI, this is, that can identify patterns in things, statistically, and therefore seek to anticipate and to forecast what might happen in certain situations and as the results of certain actions. AI involving neural language processing, that shapes the responses of such assistants as Siri and Alexa and assists in the kind of translation work that C-3PO of *Stars Wars* fame was proudly aware. Machines that learn enough, from the data they mine and the patterns they detect, to suggest songs you might like or films or games or vacations or articles you might read related to the topic you are researching. And LLMs, that are designed to process language, retrieve, recognize, classify and—encouraged and guided by our prompts—arrange text to create what we would regard in its appearance, and possibly more, as creative writing.

When thinking about creative writing, which is writing with the heightened contribution, stimulation, and guidance of our individual human imaginations the questions posed by the evolution and use of AI are not merely technical ones. These questions are likewise not only questions of whether the end results of using AI are works we recognize as, say, novels or poems of screenplays. Rather, the questions posed by the AI in creative writing relate to what we believe creative writing to be—not only its material presence, but the actions we undertake and the thoughts and the imaginative leaps and the emotional contexts and the environmental influences and the personal presence of us, as individual writers, and the cultural background and societal influences. Questions, that is, of how human creative writing happens to be and whether the use of AI to undertake it takes any of that away or, alternatively perhaps, whether it enhances it.

Graeme Harper

Index

G. Harper (ed.), *AI and Creative Writing*,
https://doi.org/10.1007/978-3-031-99101-1

The manufacturer's authorised representative in the EU is Springer
Nature Customer Service Centre GmbH, Europaplatz 3, 69115 Heidelberg,
Germany. If you have any concerns regarding our products, please
contact ProductSafety@springernature.com

Printed and bound by CPI Group (UK) Ltd, Croydon, CR0 4YY
21/09/2026
02219945-0001